The Jacobite Rebellions (1689-1746)
(Bell's Scottish History Source Books.)

D1133545

J. Pringle Thomson

Alpha Editions

This edition published in 2022

ISBN: 9789356158863

Design and Setting By

Alpha Editions

www.alphaedis.com

Email - info@alphaedis.com

Table of Contents

EDITOR'S NOTE

Within the compass of 120 pages it was impossible for me to cover every event in this period. The "Forty-Five" itself would have provided enough material to fill a volume of double the size. I have therefore concentrated on the four events which seemed to me most important—namely, the Darien scheme, the Union of the Crowns, and the risings of 1715 and 1745. For the rest, I have endeavoured to illustrate, however briefly, the religious, social, and industrial activities of the time. As in my previous volume, I have drawn freely on the invaluable publications of the Scottish Historical Society, and my thanks are also due to Mr. William Cowan for permission to print the extract which appears on p. 29.

GLASGOW,
May, 1914.

STATE OF PARTIES IN SCOTLAND (1689)

Source.—*Memoirs of Great Britain and Ireland, from the Dissolution of the Last Parliament of Charles II. until the Sea-Battle off La Hogue,* vol. i., p. 215, by Sir John Dalrymple, Bart. (London and Edinburgh: 1771.)

Of those who had offered their services to William for the settlement of Scotland, three were eminent above the rest: the Duke of Hamilton, the Marquis of Athole, and Lord Stair. The Duke of Hamilton had disapproved of the measures of the late reign, but without publicly opposing them. He had observed the same cautious conduct with regard to the parties of his countrymen. He took advantage of his rank to attend none of those public cabals in which all party-measures had been conducted in Scotland, from the time of the tables of the covenant; and, by that singularity, appeared to be of no party, at the same time when he was dealing in private with all parties. Son of the illustrious house of Douglas, married to the heiress of the house of Hamilton, related to the royal family, and to most of the crowned heads of Europe, in succession in right of his wife to the crown of Scotland, at a time when the ancient families of Scotland were of importance in the scale of government, because they were of importance in their own country, his pre-eminence was seen by William, and perhaps feared. He had been entrusted with none of the secrets of the revolution from the ambiguity of his conduct. Yet he took a violent side against King James upon his first retreat, but made apologies to that Prince's friends, so soon as he heard of his return. William, therefore, affected to show him the highest honours, cajolling him by those arts which the Duke was in use to employ upon others. From hence, and from the vanity of pre-eminence, he had consented to preside in the Assembly at London, which offered the Prince the administration of government. And hence, William gave him all the influence of the court, to be president of that convention which was to make the offer of government itself.

The Marquis of Athole was a subject of great consequence, because his estate and power lay in the heart of the highlands. He had concurred in all the measures of the two royal brothers, and had been loaded with favours and honours by both. Yet, upon news of James's retreat, he flew, from restlessness of temper more than from principle, to London, while Scotland was yet in disquiet; resolved, amid contending Princes, to make the best terms for himself. He almost alone, of all those who went to London to offer their service to the Prince of Orange, returned home discontented; because his views had been too sanguine, and because he was ashamed of what he had done. His repentance he made offer of to the friends of James in Scotland, which was received, and thanked in public, but in secret distrusted.

Lord Stair had none of the external advantages of the other two. Yet, from great reach of thought, and through knowledge of men and parties gained from experience, he came to be a considerable figure in party.... Upon the restoration he attached himself to the Duke of Lauderdale. The furies of that minister he often moderated, and often opposed, openly when he could, secretly when he could not; yet still preserved his friendship. After enduring many years the loss of his rank and his country, from the injustice of the Duke of York, he, at the age of seventy, assumed again his long-neglected sword and cuirass, and came over with the Prince of Orange, who was so fond of him that he carried him in his own ship. The influence of Lord Stair in party was increased by that of his son Sir John Dalrymple, a man distinguished above all by the beauty of his person, and the power of his eloquence. To the wisdom and experience of the father, to the parts and show of the son, rather than to the power of the Duke of Hamilton, William, certain that the two former could never hope to be pardoned by James, resolved to leave the management of Scotland in the end; but, in the meantime, to make advantage of the Duke's offers of service for the settlement of that country.

Of all those nobles whom James, when Duke of York, had honoured with his friendship, and when King, graced with his favours, a few only continued openly in his interest. Of these the chief were the Duke of Gordon, a Roman Catholic, to whom James had entrusted the castle of Edinburgh, a man weak, and wavering in courage, but bound by shame and religion; Lord Balcarres attached by affection, gratitude, and that delicacy of sentiment which the love of letters commonly inspires; and Lord Dundee, who had for ever before his eyes ideas of glory, the duty of a soldier, and the example of the great Montrose, from whose family he was descended. James had entrusted the care of his civil concerns in Scotland to Balcarres, and of his military ones to Dundee. William asked both to enter into his service. Dundee refused without ceremony. Balcarres confessed the trust which had been put in him, and asked the King, if, after that, he could enter into the service of another? William generously answered, "I cannot say that you can." But added, "Take care that you fall not within the law; for otherwise I shall be forced against my will to let the law overtake you." The other nobles of the late King's party waited for events, in hopes and in fears from the old government and the new, intriguing with both, and depended upon by neither.

THE CONVENTION OF ESTATES (1689)

Source.—*Memoirs of Great Britain and Ireland, from the Dissolution of the Last Parliament of Charles II. until the Sea-Battle off La Hogue*, vol. i., p. 218, by Sir John Dalrymple, Bart. (London and Edinburgh: 1771.)

The convention met on the 14th of March. As the governing part of the boroughs had been modelled by King James, the members sent up from thence should have been favourable to his interests. But Lord Stair, whose views were extensive, had taken care, in the paper which contained the offer of administration to the Prince, to recommend that the borough-elections should be made by a general poll of the burgesses; an artifice which, while it took the blame of innovation off the Prince, prepared the way for securing the elections to the whigs and presbyterians. The parties at the convention first tried their strengths in the choice of a president. The Duke of Hamilton was set up by the new, the Marquis of Athole by the old court: a singular situation, where both candidates were distrusted, both by those who recommended, and by those who elected them. The former was preferred by 40 votes out of about 150 voters: a victory which, from the nature of the human mind, determined the wavering. A committee of elections was next named, consisting of nine whigs and three tories. Sir John Dalrymple, who was an able lawyer, found it easy to start objections to the returns of the opposite party, and to remove those which were made against his own. The committee in the house followed his opinions, because the necessity of the times was made the excuse of partiality....

When the convention sat down, two letters were presented, one from the present, and another from the late King of England. The convention read both; but first passed an act, that nothing contained in the last of them should dissolve their assembly, or stop their proceeding to the settlement of the nation. James's letter was written in the terms of a conqueror and a priest; threatening the convention with punishment in this world, and damnation in the next. And, as it was counter-signed by Lord Melfort, a papist, and a minister abhorred by the presbyterians, the style and the signature hurt equally the interest which the letter was intended to serve. No answer was given. William's letter, on the contrary, was answered in strains of gratitude and respect; a distinction which sufficiently showed what might be expected with regard to the future resolutions of the assembly....

The revolution in England was brought about by a coalition of whigs and tories; but, in Scotland, by the whigs almost alone. Hence, the Scottish convention, instead of amusing themselves with school disputes about words, which, while they discovered the fine lines of party in England, had embarrassed the English convention, struck their blow without ceremony, and came to a resolution, that King James had, by his evil deeds, *forfaulted* his right to the crown; a term which, in the language of the law of Scotland, involved in it the exclusion of all his posterity as well as his own. But, as this resolution would have comprehended the other children of James, as well as the young Prince, they agreed upon the following explanation of the word *forfaulted*. "Agreed, that the word *forfault*, in the resolution, should imply no other alteration in the succession to the crown than the seclusion of King James, the pretended Prince of Wales, and the children that shall be procreated of either of their bodies." Only five opposed these resolutions....

The convention next made offer of the crown to William and Mary: a vote in which the Duke of Queensberry and the Marquis of Athole concurred, although they had refused to be present at the other. They reconciled their conduct by saying, "That, since the throne was declared vacant by the nation, they knew none so worthy to fill it as the Prince and Princess of Orange"— a mixture of sentiment, intended to please both Kings, but which, like most compliments of the kind, pleased neither. From an excess of zeal which betrayed the cause of it, the Duke of Hamilton demeaned himself to act the part of a clerk; reading, at the ordinary place of proclamation, the act of convention aloud to the mean multitude, who found even their own vanity hurt in the sacrifice which was made to it by the first man in the nation. With more dignity the parliament accompanied the offer of the crown with such a declaration of rights as laid open all the invasions upon the constitution, not of the late King alone, but of his brother, and ascertained every disputed pretension between the crown and the subject; for, accustomed either to trample upon their sovereigns, or to be trampled upon by them, the Scottish nation chose to leave nothing to be adjusted afterwards by the vibration between the executive and legislative powers, which had kept the English constitution almost continually in a just medium between the imperiousness of the crown and the licentiousness of the subject. The Earl of Argyle for the peers, Sir James Montgomery for the knights, and Sir John Dalrymple for the boroughs, were sent to London with the offer of the crown....

The administration of the coronation-oath of Scotland was a ceremony attended with much awe; the King holding up his right hand high, whilst he swore, and repeated each word with slowness after the person who read it. It contained a clause, that the King should root out heretics. At these words, William stopt the Earl of Argyle, who was administering the oath, and declared, he did not mean to oblige himself to become a persecutor. The commissioners answering, that such was not the meaning of the oath: "Then," said the King, "I take it in that sense only." Whether this scruple was the effect of affectation or of delicacy, is immaterial: it became a King, and it pleased the people.

DUNDEE'S REBELLION (1689)

Source.—*Memoirs of the War carried on in Scotland and Ireland, 1689-1691,* by Major-General Hugh Mackay, Commander-in-Chief of His Majesty's forces. *With an appendix of original papers*, p. 225. (Edinburgh: Bannatyne Club, 1833.)

THE DUKE OF HAMILTON TO LORD MELVILL.

Holyroodhous, 8 June, 1689.

Yesternight I received your lordship's of the 4th instant, with one to General Major Mackay; I did the same night send one to the west to dispatch some to Ireland for intelligence, and write two several ways to the captains of our ships to go to the coast of Ireland to cruise there, and give the best account they could if there was any appearance of an invasion from thence, which, I am confident, there is little fears of, if it be not by the French fleet, and it's very strange if they can be able to come to our coasts and land men, if there be an English and Dutch fleet at sea as you write, but if they should be able to land any considerable force we should be in an ill condition, considering how disaffected all the north is, and if we should absolutely with all his forces recall Mackay before he dissipates or beats Dundee, all that country generally, lowlands as well as highlands, would be in arms with him; so, upon communicating your letter to the Council this morning, they thought it not fit absolutely to recall him, but leave it much to himself, and desired him to send any of the English horse that is with him to the west country, where they can be best provided with horse meat, and most of our own new levied horse we intend should go there also, and some regiments of our foot lays there and about Stirling, the rest being in St. Johnston, Dundie, and about this place, beside what is with Mackay, from whom we have not heard since what I sent you.

P. 248. THE SAME TO THE SAME.

Holyroodhous, 28 July, 1689.

MY LORD,—On Friday last Major General Mackay marched from St. Johnston with about 4000 foot, 4 troops of horse and dragoons, and was at Dunkell that night, where he received intelligence that Dundie was come to Blair in Atholl; he marched on Saturday towards him, and within two miles of Blair about 5 at night they engaged, and by several inferior officers and soldiers that is come here this evening, gives us the account, that after a sharp engagement Dundie being much stronger, the Major General was quite defeat, and I have yet heard of no officers of quality that is come of but Lieutenant Colonel Lauther, who my Lord Ruthven spoke with as he came from St. Johnston this day, and gives the same account of their being wholly routed, but the confusion is such here that the particulars is hardly to be got. We have given orders at Council this afternoon to draw all the standing forces to Stirling, and has sent to the west country to raise all the fencible men, and Sir John Lanier has write to the English forces in Northumberland to march in here, and is going to Stirling to command, for Mackay is either killed or taken by all the account we have yet got, but you shall quickly have another flying packet or an express.

THE BATTLE OF KILLIECRANKIE (1689)

Source.—*Memoirs of the War carried on in Scotland and Ireland, 1689-1691*, by Major-General Hugh Mackay, Commander-in-Chief of His Majesty's forces. *With an appendix of original papers*, p. 50. (Edinburgh: Bannatyne Club, 1833.)

Being come up to the advanced party he saw some small parties of the enemy, the matter of a short mile, marching slowly along the foot of a hill which lay towards Blair, marching towards us; whereupon he sent orders to Balfour to march up to him in all haste with the foot. But presently upon that order, having discovered some bodies of them marching down an high hill, within a quarter of a mile to the place where he stood, when the gross of their body appeared, fearing that they should take possession of an eminence just above the ground where our forces halted on, of a steep and difficult ascent, full of trees and shrubs, and within a carbine shot of the place whereon we stood, whereby they could undoubtedly force us with their fire in confusion over the river, he galloped back in all haste to the forces, and having made every battalion form by a Quart de Conversion to the right upon the ground they stood, made them march each before his face up the hill, by which means he prevented that inconveniency, and got a ground fair enough to receive the enemy, but not to attack them, there being, within a short musket shot to it, another eminence before our front, as we stood when we were up the lowest hill, near the river, whereof Dundee had already got possession before we could be well up, and had his back to a very high hill, which is the ordinary maxim of Highlanders, who never fight against regular forces upon anything of equal terms, without a sure retreat at their back, particularly if their enemies be provided of horse; and to be sure of their escape, in case of a repulse, they attack bare footed, without any clothing but their shirts, and a little Highland doublet, whereby they are certain to outrun any foot, and will not readily engage where horse can follow the chase any distance.... Shortly thereafter, and about half an hour before sunset, they began to move down the hill.

The General had already commanded the officers, commanding battalions, to begin their firing at the distance of 100 paces by platoons, to discourage the approaching Highlanders, meeting with continual fire: That part of their forces which stood opposite to Hastings, who had the right of all, before the Generals', Levin's and Kenmore's regiments, came down briskly together with their horse, and notwithstanding of a brisk fire, particularly from the General's own battalion, whereby many of the chief gentlemen of the name of Macdonald, who attacked it, were killed, pushed their point, after they had fired their light pieces at some distance, which made little or no execution, with sword in hand, tho' in great confusion, which is their usual way. Which when the General observed, he called to the Lord Belhaven to march up with the first troop of horse, ordering him to flank to the left hand the enemy, the fire being then past on all hands, and coming to handy strokes if our men had stood, appointing the second troop to do the same to the right; but scarcely had Belhaven got them without the front of the line, where they had orders to wheel for the flank, tho' their very appearance made the enemy turn away from the place where they saw the horse coming up, but contrary to orders, they began to pass, not knowing whereat, and presently turned about, as did also Kenmore's and the half of Levin's battalion.

The General, observing the horse come to a stand, and firing in confusion, and the foot beginning to fall away from him, thinking happily that the horse would be picked to follow his example, and in all cases to disengage himself out of the crowd of Highlanders which came down just upon the place where he was calling to the officers of the horse to follow him, spurr'd his horse through the enemy, (where no body nevertheless followed him, but one of his servants, whose horse was shot in passing).... Having passed through the crowd of attacking Highlanders, he turned about to see how matters stood, and found that all his left had given way, and got down the hill which was behind our line, ranged a little above the brow thereof, so that in the twinkling of an eye in a manner, our men, as well as the enemy, were out of sight, being got down pall mall to the river where our baggage stood....

The enemy lost on the field six for our one, the fire to our right having been continued and brisk, whereby not only Dundee, with several gentlemen of quality of the countys of Angus and Perth, but also many of the best gentlemen among the Highlanders, particularly of the Macdonalds of the Isles and Glengarie, were killed, coming down the hill upon Hastings, the General, and Levin's regiments, which made the best fire and all the execution....

The General having got the small rests of his forces safely over the river, and seeing no disposition, so far as he could discern, of the enemy to pursue him, he bethought himself which way he had best retire; and notwithstanding of the contrary advice of all the officers who would have him to descend the plain country of Athole to Dunkeld and Perth, he resolved rather to march into the Highlands three or four miles, and then over to Strath Tay and along the foot of the hills, over the Castle of Drummond, where he had a garrison, to Stirling, whither he resolved to make all the speed possible, to fall upon some present measures.

FOOTNOTES:

Major-General Mackay, commanding the Royal troops.

Bulk.

THE RELIGIOUS SETTLEMENT (1690)

Source.—*Letters and State Papers chiefly Addressed to George, Earl of Melville, Secretary of State for Scotland, 1689-1691*, p. 436. (Edinburgh: Bannatyne Club, 1843.)

22 May, 1690

WILLIAM R.

HIS MAJESTIES REMARQUES upon the Act for settling Church Government in Scotland, Which, together with some reasons designed for the clearing of it, and answering those objections that might be made against it, was sent to him by My Lord Commissioner.

1st, Whereas it is said that the Church of Scotland was reformed from Poperie, *by Presbyters without Prelacy*, his Majesty thinks, that tho this matter of fact may be true, which he doth not contradict, yet it being denied by some who discourse much of a power that Superintendents had in the beginning of the Reformation, which was like to that which Bishops afterwards had, it were better it were otherwise expressed.

2d, Whereas it is said that their Majesties do ratify the Presbyterial Church Government *to be the only Government of Christ's Church in this kingdom*; his Majesty desires it may be expressed thus,—to be the government of the Church in this Kingdom established by law.

3d, Whereas it is said that the government is to be exercised by sound Presbyterians, and such as for hereafter shall be owned by Presbyterian Church Judicatories, *as such*; his Majesty thinks that the rule is too general, depending as to its application upon the opinions of particular men; and therefore he desires that what is said to be the meaning of the rule in the reasons sent to him, may be expressed in the Act, viz., That such as shall subscribe to the Confession of Faith and Catechisms, and are willing to submit to the government of the Church, as established by law, being sober in their lives, sound in their doctrine, and qualified with gifts for the ministry, shall be admitted to the government, and his Majesty doth judge that the following Declaration might be a good Test:—

I, A—— B—— do sincerely declare, and promise, that I will own and submit to the present government of the Church, as it is now by Law established in this Kingdom, and that I will heartily concur with and under it, for the suppressing of sin and wickedness, the promoting of piety, and the purging of the Church of all erroneous and scandalous Ministers; and I do also assent and consent to the Confession of Faith, and the Larger and

Shorter Catechisms, now confirmed by Act of Parliament, as the Standard of the Protestant religion in this Kingdom.

... 5th, As to what concerns the meeting of Synods and General Assemblies, his Majesty is willing that it should be enacted, that they meet at such and such times of the year, and as often as shall be judged necessary, provided always, that they apply to him or his Privy Council to know if there be any inconveniency as to public affairs in their meeting at such times, and have his allowance accordingly; and that in all their General Assemblies, a Commissioner in the name of his Majesty be there present, to the end, that nothing may be proposed, but what merely concerns the Church; and in case anything relating to the Civil government, or that is prejudicial to it, should be there proposed or debated, the said Commissioner may give a stop to it, till he has acquainted the Privy Council, and received their direction in it.

6th, Whereas it is desired to be enacted, that the parishes of those thrust out by the people in the beginning of this Revolution be declared Vacant upon this reason, *because they were put upon congregations without their consent,* his Majesty desires it may be so expressed, as may be consistent with the rights of Patrons, which he thinks he hath the more reason to desire, because in the reasons sent up with the Act, it seems to be acknowledged that this procedure is Extraordinary, and not to be drawn into consequence....

His Majesties resolution to be candid and above board in what he does, and his desire, that what is now granted by him to the Church may not be uneasie to him afterwards, do incline him to have the above-mentioned amendments in the Act.

It is his Majesties desire, that such as are of the Episcopal persuasion in Scotland have the same Indulgence that Dissenters have in England, provided they give security to live peaceably under the Government, and take the Oath of Allegiance.

THE MASSACRE OF GLENCOE (1692)

Source.—*Papers Illustrative of the Political Condition of the Highlands of Scotland from the Year 1689 to 1696*, p. 68. (Glasgow: Maitland Club, 1845.)

A. SIR THO. LIVINGSTOUN, COMMANDER-IN-CHIEF IN SCOTLAND TO COLL. HAMILTON AT FORT WILLIAM.

Edr., 23d Jary. 92.

SIR,—Since my last I understand that the Laird of Glenco, coming after the prefixed time, was not admitted to take the oath, which is very good news here, being that at Court it's wished he had not taken it, so that that [th]eiving nest might be entirely rooted out; for the Secretary in three of his last letters hath made mention of him, and it is known at Court he has not taken it. So Sir, here is a fair occasion for you to show that your garrison serves for some use; and being that the orders are so positive from Court to me not to spare [a]n[y] of them that have not timely come in, as you may by the orders I sent to your Col., I desire you would begin with Glenco, and spair nothing which belongs to him, but do not trouble the Government with prisoners. I shall expect to hear what progress you have made in this, and remain, Sir, Your humble Servant

B. FOR HIS MAJESTIES SERVICE TO CAPTAIN ROBERT CAMPBELL OF GLENLYON (*idem*, p. 72).

1692, Feb. 12.

SIR,—You are hereby ordered to fall upon the rebels, the M'Donalds of Glenco, and to put all to the sword under 70. You are to have a special care that the old fox and his sones do not escape your hands. You are to secure

- 13 -

all the avenues, that no man escape. This you are to put in execution at fyve of the clock precisely. And by that time, or very shortly after it, I will strive to be at yow with a stronger party. If I do not come to yow at fyve, you are not to tarry for me, but to fall on. This by the King's special commands, for the good and safety of the country, that these miscreants be cutt off root and branch. So that this be put in execution without feed or favour, as you may expect to be dealt with as one not true to King nor country, nor a man fit to carry commission in the King's service. Expecting ye will not fail in the fulfilling hereof, as yow love yourself, I subscryve this with my hand at Ballacholis, 12 febrry, 1692

C. REPORT OF THE COMMISSION GIVEN BY HIS MAJESTY, UNDER THE GREAT SEAL, 29TH APRIL, 1695, FOR INQUIRING INTO THE SLAUGHTER OF THE MEN OF GLENCO, 13TH FEBRUARY, 1692 (*idem*, p. 99).

At Holyrudhouse, 20th June, 1695.

... The things to be remark'd preceding the said slaughter were, that it's certain that the Lairds of Glenco and Auchintriaten, and their followers, were in the insurrection and rebellion made by some of the Highland clans, under the command, first of the Viscount of Dundee, and then of Major-Gen. Buchan, in the years 1689 and 1690. This is acknowledg'd by all. But when the Earl of Breadalbane called the heads of the clans, and met with them at Auchallader, in July 1691, in order to a cessation, the deceas'd Alexander Macdonald of Glenco was there, with Glengary, Sir John Maclene, and others, and agreed to the cessation; as it is also acknowledg'd.... And here the Commissioners cannot but take notice of what hath occurr'd to them in two letters from Secretary Stair, to Lieutenant-Colonel Hamilton, one of the 1st, and another of the 3d of December, 1691, wherein he expresses his resentment from the marring of the bargain that should have been betwixt the Earl of Breadalbane and the Highlanders, to a very great height; ... — And, in effect, seems, even at that time, which was almost a month before the expiring of the King's indemnity, to project, with Lieutenant-Colonel Hamilton, that some of them should be rooted out and destroyed. His Majesty's proclamation of indemnity was publish'd in Aug. 1691, offering a free indemnity and pardon to all the Highlanders who had been in arms, upon their coming in, and taking the oath of allegiance, betwixt then and the first of January thereafter: And, in compliance with the proclamation, the deceas'd Glenco goes, about the end of Decemb. 1691, to Col. Hill, Governor of Fort William at Inverlochie, and desir'd the Colonel to minister to him the oath of allegiance, that he might have the King's indemnity: But Col. Hill, in his deposition, doth further depone, that he hasten'd him away all he could, and gave him a letter to Ardkinlas to receive him as a lost sheep; ... Sir Colin Campbell of Ardkinlas, Sherif-Deput of Argyle, depones, that the deceas'd Glenco came to Inverary about the beginning of January, 1692, with a letter from Colonel Hill, to the effect above mentioned, and was three days there before Ardkinlas could get thither, because of bad weather; and that Glenco said to him, that he had not come sooner because he was hinder'd by the storm; and Ardkinlas farther depones, that when he declin'd to give the oath of allegiance to Glenco, because the last of December, the time appointed for the taking of it, was past, Glenco begg'd, with tears, that he might be admitted to take it, and promis'd to bring in all his people within a short time to do the like, and, if any of them refused, they should be imprisoned, or sent to Flanders: upon which, Ardkinlas says, he did administer to him the oath of allegiance upon the 6th of January, 1692....

These things having preceded the slaughter, which happen'd not to be committed until the 13th of February, 1692, six weeks after the deceas'd Glenco had taken the oath of allegiance at Inverary. The slaughter of the Glenco men was in this manner, viz., John and Alexander MacDonalds, sons to the deceas'd Glenco, depone, that Glengary's house being reduc'd, the forces were called back to the south, and Glenlyon, a captain of the Earl of Argyle's regiment, with Lieutenant Lindsay, and Ensign Lindsay, and six score soldiers, return'd to Glenco about the 1st of February, 1692, where, at their entry, the elder brother, John, met them, with about 20 men, and demanded the reason of their coming; and Lieutenant Lindsay showed him his orders for quartering there, under Colonel Hill's hand, and gave assurance that they were only come to quarter; whereupon they were billeted in the country, and had free quarters, and kind entertainment, living familiarly with the people until the 13th day of Feb.; and Alexander farther depones, that Glenlyon, being his wife's uncle, came almost every day, and took his morning drink at his house, and that the very night before the slaughter,

Glenlyon did play at cards, in his own quarters, with both the brothers; and John depones, that old Glenco, his father, had invited Glenlyon, Lieutenant Lindsay, and Ensign Lindsay, to dine with him upon the very day the slaughter happened. But, on the 13th day of February, being Saturday, about four, or five, in the morning, Lieutenant Lindsay, with a party of the foresaid soldiers, came to old Glenco's house, where, having call'd, in a friendly manner, and got in, they shot his father dead, with several shots, as he was rising out of his bed; and, the mother having got up, and put on her clothes, the soldiers stripp'd her naked, and drew the rings off her fingers with their teeth; as likewise they killed one man more, and wounded another grievously, at the same place.... And the said John, Alexander, and Archibald MacDonalds, do all depone, that, the same morning, there was one Sergeant Barber, and a party, at Auchnaion, and that Auchintriaten being there, in his brother's house, with eight more, sitting about the fire, the soldiers discharged upon them about 18 shot, which killed Auchintriaten, and four more; ... And, at Innerriggin, where Glenlyon was quartered, the soldiers took other nine men, and did bind them, hand and foot, [and] kill'd them, one by one, with shot; and, when Glenlyon inclin'd to save a young man, of about 20 years of age, one Captain Drummond came, and ask'd how he came to be sav'd in respect of the orders that were given, and shot him dead; and another young boy, of about 13 years, ran to Glenlyon, to be sav'd. He was likewise shot dead.... And all these five witnesses concur, that the aforesaid slaughter was made by Glenlyon, and his soldiers, after they had been quarter'd, and liv'd peaceably, and friendly, with the Glenco men about 13 days, and that the number of those whom they knew to be slain were about 25, and that the soldiers, after the slaughter, did burn the houses, barns, and goods, and carried away a great spoil of horse, nolt, and sheep, above a 1,000.

... And upon the whole matter, it is the opinion of the Commission, First, that it was a great wrong that Glenco's case, and diligence as to his taking the oath of allegiance, with Ardkinlas's certificate of his taking the oath of allegiance on the 6th of January, 1692, and Col. Hill's letter to Ardkinlas, and Ardkinlas's letter to Colin Campbell, Sheriff-Clerk, for clearing Glenco's diligence and innocence, were not presented to the Lords of his Majesty's Privy Council, when they were sent into Edinburgh, in the said month of January, and that those who advis'd the not presenting thereof were in the wrong, and seem to have had a malicious design against Glenco; ... Secondly, that it appears to have been known at London, and particularly to the Master of Stair, in the month of January, 1692, that Glenco had taken the oath of allegiance, tho' after the day prefix'd; for he saith, in his letter of the 30th of January, to Sir Tho. Livingston, as is above remark'd, "I am glad that Glenco came not in within the time prescrib'd." Thirdly, that there was nothing in the King's instructions to warrant the committing of the foresaid slaughter, even as to the thing it self, and far less as to the manner of it, seeing all his instructions do plainly import, that the most obstinate of the rebels might be received into mercy upon taking the oath of allegiance, tho' the day was long before elaps'd, and that he ordered nothing concerning Glenco and his tribe, but that "if" they could "be well separated from the rest, it" would "be a proper indication of the publick justice to extirpate that sept of thieves"; which plainly intimates, that it was his Majesty's mind that they could not be separated from the rest of these rebels, unless they still refused his mercy by continuing in arms and refusing the allegiance, and that, even in that case, they were only to be proceeded against in the way of publick justice, and no other way.

FOOTNOTES:

Of allegiance to King William.

The Master of Stair.

Probably fear.

Ballachulish.

Cattle.

THE BANK OF SCOTLAND (1695)

Source.—*The Acts of the Parliaments of Scotland*, vol. ix., p. 495. (London: 1822.)

ACT FOR ERECTING A PUBLICK BANK.

Our Sovereign Lord considering how useful a Publick Bank may be in this Kingdom according to the custom of other kingdoms and states, and that the same can only be best set up and managed by persons in company with a Joynt Stock, sufficiently endowed with these powers and authorities and liberties necessary and usual in such cases, Hath therefore allowed, and with the advice and consent of the Estates of Parliament allows, a joynt stock amounting to the sum of twelve hundred thousand pounds money to be raised by the Company hereby established for the carrying on and managing of a publick bank. And further statutes and ordains, with advice foresaid, that the persons under-named ... shall have power to appoint a Book for subscriptions of persons, either natives or foreigners, who shall be willing to subscribe and pay into the joynt stock, Which subscriptions the foresaids persons or their quorum are hereby authorized to receive in the foresaid book, which shall lie open every tuesday or friday from nine to twelve in the forenoon, and from three to six in the afternoon betwixt the first day of November next and the first day of January next following, in the publick hall or chamber to be appointed in the City of Edinburgh. And therein all persons shall have liberty to subscribe for such sums of money as they shall think fit to adventure in the said joynt stock, one thousand pound Scots being the lowest sum, and twenty thousand pound Scots the highest. And the two third parts of the saids stocks belonging always to persons residing in Scotland. Likeas, each and every person at the time of his subscribing shall pay into the hands of the fore-named persons, or any three of them, ten of the hundred of the sums set down in their respective subscriptions towards the carrying on the Bank. And all and every the persons subscribing and paying into the said stock, as aforsaid, shall be and are hereby declared to be one Body Corporat and Politique, by the name of THE GOVERNOUR AND COMPANY OF THE BANK OF SCOTLAND, under which name they shall have perpetual succession, and shall have a Common Seal....

And it is farder hereby statute and ordained that it shall be lawful for the said Governour and Company to lend, upon real or personal security, any sum or sums, and to receive annual rent for the same at six per cent., as shall be ordinary for the time. As also, that if the person borrowing as said is, shall not make payment at the time agreed upon with the Company, then it shall be lawful for the Governour and Company to sell and dispose of the security or pledge by a public roup, for the most that can be got for payment to them of the principal annual rents and reasonable charges, and returning the over-plus to the person who gave the said security or pledge....

It is hereby statute that the joynt stock of the said Bank, continuing in money, shall be free from all publick burdens to be imposed upon money for the space of twenty one years after the date hereof. And that during this space it shall not be leisom to any other persons to enter into and set up ane distinct Company of Bank within this Kingdom, besides these persons allennarly in whose favour this Act is granted.... And it is likeways hereby provided that all foreigners who shall join as partners of this Bank shall thereby be and become naturalized Scotsmen to all intents and purposes.

FOOTNOTES:

Lawful.

Only.

THE DARIEN SCHEME (1695-1700)
A. THE PROJECT AND ITS ORIGINATOR (1695)

Source.—Bishop Burnet's *History of His Own Times*, vol. iv., p. 282. (Oxford: 1833.)

Another act passed, that has already produced very fatal consequences to that kingdom; and may yet draw worse after it: the interlopers in the East India trade, finding that the company was like to be favoured by the parliament, as well as by the court, were resolved to try other methods to break in upon that trade: they entered into a treaty with some merchants in Scotland; and they had, in the former session, procured an act, that promised letters patents to all such as should offer to set up new manufactures, or drive any new trade, not yet practised by that kingdom, with an exemption for twenty-one years from all taxes and customs, and with all such other privileges, as should be found necessary for establishing or encouraging such projects. But here was a necessity of procuring letters patents, which they knew the credit that the East India company had at court would certainly render ineffectual. So they were now in treaty for a new act, which should free them from that difficulty.

There was one Paterson, a man of no education, but of great notions; which, as was generally said, he had learned from the Buccaneers, with whom he had consorted for some time. He had considered a place in Darien, where he thought a good settlement might be made, with another over against it, in the South Sea; and by two settlements there, he fancied a great trade might be opened both for the East and West Indies; and that the Spaniards in the neighbourhood might be kept in great subjection to them; so he made the merchants believe, that he had a great secret, which he did not think fit yet to discover, and reserved to a fitter opportunity; only he desired, that the West Indies might be named in any new act that should be offered to the parliament: he made them in general understand, that he knew of a country, not possessed by Spaniards, where there were rich mines, and gold in abundance. While these matters were in treaty, the time of the King's giving the instructions to his commissioner for the parliament came on; and it had been a thing of course, to give a general instruction, to pass all bills for the encouragement of trade. Johnstoun told the King, that he heard there was a secret management among the merchants for an act in Scotland, under which the East India trade might be set up; so he proposed, and drew an instruction, impowering the commissioner to pass any bill, promising letters patents for encouraging of trade, yet limited, so that it should not interfere with the trade of England: when they went down to Scotland, the King's commissioner either did not consider this, or had no regard to it; for he gave the royal assent to an act, that gave the undertakers, either of the East India or West India trade, all possible privileges, with exemption of twenty-one years from all impositions: and the act directed letters patents to be passed under the great seal, without any further warrant for them: when this was printed, it gave a great alarm in England, more particularly to the East India company; for many of the merchants of London resolved to join stock with the Scotch company; and the exemption from all duties gave a great prospect of gain. Such was the posture of affairs in Scotland....

Great complaints were made in both houses of the act for the Scotch East India company, and addresses were made to the King, setting forth the inconveniencies that were like to arise from thence to England: the King answered, that he had been ill served in Scotland: but he hoped remedies should be found, to prevent the ill consequences that they apprehended from the act: and soon after this, he turned out both the secretaries of state, and the marquis of Tweedale: and great changes were made in the whole ministry of that Kingdom, both high and low....

But when it was understood in Scotland that the King had disowned the act for the East India company, from which it was expected that great riches should flow into that Kingdom, it is not easy to conceive how great and how general an indignation was spread over the whole kingdom: the Jacobites saw what a game it was like to prove in their hands; they played it with great skill, and to the advantage of their cause, in a course of many years; and continue to manage it to this day: there was a great deal of noise made of the Scotch act in both houses of parliament in England, by some who seemed to have no other design in that, but to heighten our distractions by the apprehensions that they expressed. The Scotch nation fancied nothing but mountains of gold; and the credit of the design rose so high, that subscriptions were made, and advances of money were offered, beyond what any believed the wealth of that Kingdom could have furnished. Paterson came to have such credit among them, that the design of the East India trade, how promising soever, was wholly laid aside: and they resolved to employ all their wealth in the settling a colony, with a port and fortifications, in Darien; which was long kept a secret, and was only trusted to a select number, who assumed to themselves the name of the African company, though they never meddled with any concern in that part of the world; the unhappy progress of the affair will appear in its proper time.

FOOTNOTES:

Scotland.

B. Constitution of the Company (1698)

Source.—*The Darien Papers: being a Selection of Original Letters and Official Documents relating to the Establishment of a Colony at Darien by the Company of Scotland trading to Africa and the Indies, 1695-1700.* (Edinburgh: Bannatyne Club, 1849.)

Know all men by these presents, that in pursuance of the powers and privileges granted by the 32nd Act of the 4th Session and the 8th Act of the 5th Session of this current Parliament—as well as by His Majesty's letters patent under the great seal of this Kingdom, to the Company of Scotland trading to Africa and the Indies, the Council General of the said Company have upon mature deliberation *Resolved* (God willing) to settle and plant a Colony in some place or other not inhabited, in America, or in or upon any other place, by consent of the natives and inhabitants thereof, and not possessed by any European Sovereign, Potentate, Prince, or State, to be called by the name of CALEDONIA; and the said Council General, reposing full trust and confidence in the capacity, fidelity, discretion, and good conduct of their trusty and well-beloved friends, Major James Cunningham of Eickett, Mr. James Montgomery, Mr. Daniel Mackay, Cap[n] Robert Jolly, Cap[n] Robert Pennicuik, Cap[n] William Vetch, and Cap[n] Robert Pinkarton,— have Resolved and fully agreed upon the following fundamental Constitutions as a perpetual Rule of Government for the said Colony, viz.

1. That the Government Civil, Military and Admirality of the said Colony and dependancies thereof, shall be and remain in the persons of the said Major James Cunningham of Eickett, Mr. James Montgomery, Mr. Daniel Mackay, Cap[t] Robert Jolly, Cap[t] Robert Pennicuik, Cap[t] William Vetch, and Cap[t] Robert Pinkarton, from the time of their setting sail from Scotland, together with such others as shall be assum'd and added to them in manner after specified....

6. That all Persons, of what Nation soever, have full freedom and liberty to trade to and from the said colony under the condition after mentioned, and that such of them as shall come to live and inhabite on the said Colony, shall according to their respective States and conditions enjoy equal privileges with the other Inhabitants thereof, such Inhabitants first giving up their several names and designations to be enrolled in a particular Register to be kept for that use....

8. That the Company do reserve to themselves, the 1/20th part of all Lands and grounds that shall be possessed by the said Colony.

9. That the Company do also reserve to themselves, the 1/20th part of all Gold-dust, Mines of Gold, Silver, or other Metalls or Minerals, to be

delivered above ground free of all Charges, together with the said proportion of Pearl-fishing, Wrecks, Ambergreese, precious wood, Jewels, Gems or Stones of value, that shall any ways be found in or upon the said Colony or dependancies thereof, and that the remaining 19 parts thereof do equally belong to the Company and Colony in proportion to their respective proportions of Lands in the said Colony, they always contributing in proportion to their respective interests to all Charges for discovering and working the said Mines and others....

In testimony of all which Premisses, these presents are in name, presence, and by order of the said Council General, Signed by the Company's Secretary and Sealed with the Company's Seal, At Edinburgh the eighth day of July One Thousand Six hundred and Ninty eight years.

C. WHY THE COLONY FAILED (1698)

Source.—Bishop Burnet's *History of His Own Times*, vol. iv., p. 395. (Oxford: 1833.)

... The company in Scotland, this year, set out a fleet, with a colony, on design to settle in America: the secret was better kept than could have been well expected, considering the many hands in which it was lodged; it appeared at last, that the true design had been guessed, from the first motion of it: they landed at Darien, which, by the report that they sent over, was capable of being made a strong place, with a good port. It was no wonder that the Spaniards complained loudly of this; it lay so near Porto Bello and Panama on the one side, and Carthagena on the other, that they could not think they were safe, when such a neighbour came so near the centre of their Empire in America: the King of France complained also of this, as an invasion of the Spanish dominions, and offered the court of Madrid a fleet to dislodge them. The Spaniards pressed the King hard upon this: they said, they were once possessed of that place; and though they found it too unhealthy to settle there, yet the right to it belonged still to them: so this was a breach of treaties, and a violent possession of their country. In answer to this, the Scotch pretended, that the natives of Darien were never conquered by the Spaniards, and were by consequence a free people; they said, they had purchased of them leave to possess themselves of that place, and that the Spaniards abandoned the country, because they could not reduce the natives: so the pretension of the first discovery was made void, when they went off from it, not being able to hold it; and then the natives being left to themselves, it was lawful for the Scots to treat with them: it was given out, that there was much gold in the country. Certainly, the nation was so full of hopes from this project, that they raised a fund for carrying it on, greater than, as was thought, that kingdom could stretch to; four hundred thousand pounds sterling was subscribed, and a fourth part was paid down, and afterwards, seventy thousand pounds more was brought in, and a national fury seemed to have transported the whole kingdom, upon this project.

... Our English plantations grew ... very jealous of this new colony: they feared, that the double prospect of finding gold and of robbing the Spaniards, would draw many planters from them into this new settlement; and that the buccaneers might run into them: for by the Scotch act, this place was to be made a free port; and if it was not ruined before it was well formed, they reckoned it would become a seat of piracy and another Algiers in those parts. Upon these grounds, the English nation inclined to declare against this, and the King seemed convinced, that it was an infraction of his treaties with Spain: so orders were sent, but very secretly, to the English plantations, particularly to Jamaica and the Leeward islands, to forbid all commerce with the Scots at Darien. The Spaniards made some faint attempts on them, but without success. This was a very great difficulty on the King; he saw how much he was like to be pressed on both hands, and he apprehended what ill consequences were like to follow, on his declaring himself either way.

D. INDIGNATION IN SCOTLAND (1699)

Source.—Bishop Burnet's *History of His Own Times*, vol. iv., p. 429. (Oxford: 1833.)

In Scotland all men were full of hopes, that their new colony should bring them home mountains of gold; the proclamations sent to Jamaica and to the other English plantations were much complained of, as acts of hostility, and a violation of the common rights of humanity; these had a great effect on them, though without these, that colony was too weak and too ill supplied, as well as too much divided within itself, to have subsisted long; those, who had first possessed themselves of it, were forced to abandon it: soon after they had gone from it, a second recruit of men and provisions was sent thither from Scotland; but one of their ships unhappily took fire, in which they had the greatest stock of provisions; and so these likewise went off: and though the third reinforcement, that soon followed this, was both stronger and better furnished, yet they fell into such factions among themselves, that they were too weak to resist the Spaniards, who, feeble as they were, yet saw the necessity of attacking them: and they finding themselves unable to resist the force which was brought against them, capitulated; and with that the whole design fell to the ground, partly for want of stock and skill in those who managed it, and partly by the baseness and treachery of those whom they employed.

The conduct of the King's ministers in Scotland was much censured in the whole progress of this affair; for they had connived at it, if not encouraged it, in hopes that the design would fall of itself; but now it was not so easy to cure the universal discontent, which the miscarriage of this design, to the impoverishing the whole kingdom, had raised, and which now began to spread, like a contagion, among all sorts of people. A petition for a present session of parliament was immediately sent about the kingdom, and was signed by many thousands: this was sent up by some of the chief of their nobility, whom the King received very coldly: yet a session of parliament was granted them, to which the duke of Queensbury was sent down commissioner ... it was further given out, to raise the national disgust yet higher, that the opposition the King gave to the Scotch colony, flowed neither from a regard to the interests of England, nor to the treaties with Spain, but from a care of the Dutch, who from Curasoe drove a coasting trade, among the Spanish plantations, with great advantage; which, they said, the Scotch colony, if once well settled, would draw wholly from them.... In the session of parliament it was carried by a vote, to make the affair of Darien a national concern: upon that, the session was for some time discontinued. When the news of the total abandoning of Darien was brought over, it cannot be well expressed into how bad a temper this cast the body of that people: they had now lost almost two hundred thousand pounds sterling upon this project, besides all the imaginary treasure they had promised themselves from it: so the nation was raised into a sort of a fury upon it, and in the first heat of that, a remonstrance was sent about the kingdom for hands, representing to the King, the necessity for a present sitting of the parliament, which was drawn in so high a strain, as if they had resolved to pursue the effects of it by an armed force. It was signed by a great majority of the members of parliament; and the ferment in men's spirits was raised so high, that few thought it could have been long curbed, without breaking forth into great extremities.

FOOTNOTES:

Curaçoa.

THE UNION IMPENDING (1703)

Source.—*Memoirs of the Life of Sir John Clerk of Penicuik, Baronet, Baron of the Exchequer: extracted by himself from his own Journals, 1676-1755*, p. 46. (Edinburgh: Scottish Historical Society, 1892.)

A Convention of Estates followed the Revolution by King William in 1688, which was afterwards turned into a Parliament, and continued 'till the Death of that King in 1702. The same parliament continued to sit upon the accession of Queen Ann to the Crown, and was not dissolved till the year 1703, when the new Parliament was called.... I have thrown together some observations on this session of Parliament in another Manuscript book, so shall say little here. It was divided into 3 factions, who, as they had different views, drove different ways. The first was what was called the Court party; they were for supporting the Crown and the Credit of the High Commissioner, consequently they were for giving moderate subsidies for supporting the Government against the insults of the French, with whom we were, at that time, in war. They had the union of the two nations in view, because they not only considered it as the happiest thing that could be brought about for the Interest of Great Britain, but because it was expressly recommended to them by the Queen. The second faction was that of the Jacobites; they were to thwart and disturb the Administration at any rate. The third faction was what went under the name of the Squadrone Volante. These consisted of about fifteen Lords and Gentlemen, all Whigs in their principles, but who herded together, and kept little or no communication with the Duke of Queensberry and his Friends. They were for opposing everything which they durst oppose, but to keep firmly in their view the succession of the Crown in the House of Hanover. They pretended to be great Patriots, and to stand up chiefly in defence of the rights and privileges of the subjects; in a word, the public good and the liberty of the subjects were still in their mouths, but in their Hearts they were known to have Court preferments and places in the chiefest degree of veneration. These were the springs and motives of all their Actions, which appeared in a hundred instances thereafter. However, by the bye, I must say that such a Squadrone Volante in any Parliament seems to be always a happy means in the hand of Providence to keep the several members of an Administration in their duty, for people in great power seldom fail to take more upon them than falls to their share.

The chiefs of the Squadrone Lords were the Dukes of Montrose and Roxburgh, the Earls of Rothes and Haddington, all these young men of about 24 years of Age; but the chief of all, at least the man under whose name they principally voted, was the Marquis of Tweeddale, a very good Man, but not perfectly qualified for Court intrigues.

Amongst their Gentlemen was one Mr. Fletcher of Saltoun, a Man of Republican principles, who had spent his youth in Holland, had been forfeited under the late King James, but afterwards restored under King William by Act of Parliament. He was a man a little untoward in his temper, and much inclined to Eloquence. He made many speeches in Parliament, which are all printed, but was not very dexterous in making extemporary replies. He was, however, a very Honest Man, and meant well in everything he said and did, except in cases where his humour, passion, or prejudices were suffered to get the better of his reason.

FOOTNOTES:

The Royal Commissioner.

UNION OF THE CROWNS
A. The Last Scottish Parliament (1705)

Source.—*A Journey to Edenborough in Scotland*, p. 112, by Joseph Taylor, late of the Inner Temple, Esquire. Edited from the original manuscript by William Cowan. (Edinburgh: 1903.)

It hapned whilst we were at Edenborough, that the Act for a treaty of Union, between England and Scotland, was upon debate, and having the honour to have severall Lords and Members of parliament often dine with us, they inform'd us of the Grand day when the Act was to be past or rejected, and by speciall favour of my Lord high Commissioner, we had leave to stand upon the throne by his right hand: The usuall way to admit strangers is to give them a battoon; which holding in their hands, shows that they are forreigners. The Lords and Comons sit together; As soon as we heard the names call'd over, We observ'd Dukes, Marquesses, and Earles sat on the Uppermost seats on the right hand, Viscounts and Barons on the uppermost Seats of the left, The Knights of the Shires under the Dukes, Marquesses, and Earles, and the Burgesses and Commoners under the Viscounts and Barons. The Lord Chancellor under the Commissioner's Throne, The Lord Treasurer on his right hand, and the Secretary of State on his left, and directly under him the Lord Justice Clerk, and at the head of a long Table, on which is plac't the Crown, Scepter, and Sword, the Earle Marshall; The Lord high Commissioner has his Commission always before him in a velvet purse on his cushion.

When they began to debate, we observ'd that the principall leading men of the High party, or those which oppos'd the Court, were the Duke of H——, the Duke of A——, the Lord C——y, and the Lord B—a—en, and one Fletcher of Salton, who speaks well, but with a great deal of passion, The Earle of S—f—d, who is Lord C——r, is a very ingenious man, His cheif perfection, and what is most requisite for his office in the house, is resuming debates, which he does with an admirable dexterity, by giving soe happy a turn for the Interest of the party he espouses, that he generally carryes the point, without the censure of either party. The Lord high Commissioner says nothing; The Duke of Ar——e was thought, as we were told not only too young for so high a Station, but too warm to bear the Reflections of some of the leading Malcontents, but on the contrary he behav'd himself in this criticall juncture, with so sedate and even a Temper, that he justly gain'd an universall reputation, and brought the Sessions to a happy conclusion. The Lord Chancellor determines upon all debates who shall speak first, when anything is put to the vote, every member is call'd by his name, and answers singly, approven, or not approven. The grand debate this day, being about the Act for a treaty with England, many learned speeches were made on the occasion. Some were for passing no Act till England had given them satisfaction for the affront they pretended was put upon them, by the Act pass'd last Sessions in England, which not only declar'd them Aliens, but prohibited their goods, and thereby touch't them in the most sensible part. Fletcher said, that England could not make them Aliens, since they were naturall born subjects to the Queen; ... After his debate, others were for making the English Aliens in Scotland, as a Retaliation for our making them soe in England: ... But after many other debates, and hard reflections on the English, it was at last put to the Vote, whether there should be added a clause to the Act of treaty, which should prohibit any treaty with England, till England had rescinded the Clause of Aliens, or whether it should be in a seperate way. Seperate way was carry'd by two Voices, ... The next great point was, whether the Queen or parliament should have nomination of Commissioners: ... 'Twas carry'd the Queen should nominate by 4 Voices. Then a Gentleman propos'd to add a clause, to preserve the discipline and Worship of the Kirk of Scotland, as at present establish'd: One propos'd it should be the Religion and Discipline, but my Lord Chancellor told them, that was all the same thing, and H——— said, 'twas not worth a Vote, and his brother the Earl of R——— ask't whether they might not add the Lord's prayer and Creed, and indeed by what I could observe, they would add the whole Common Liturgy of the Church of England, for they seem'd to be quite tir'd of the Kirk discipline: Now the whole Act being finish'd, the Vote was put whether it should be carry'd approven, or no, and 'twas carry'd approven, by 34 voices. As soon as this was over, we left the house, and that night Collonell Ogilby, the Lord Chancellor's brother, the Lord Hardress, and severall Lords and parliament men, came to our lodgings, and embrac'd us with all the outward marks of love and kindness, and seem'd mightily pleas'd at what was done; and told us we should now be no more English and Scotch, but Brittons. And thus we merrily spent the night, in drinking to the Success of the treaty and happy union, and next day, Colonell Ogilby and some Scotch Lords enquir'd mightily for the 3 English Gentlemen, as they call'd us, having a mind to give us a chirrupping Cup, but we went to Leith that day, being willing to avoid them.

FOOTNOTES:

Hamilton.

Athole.

Cromarty.

Belhaven.

Seafield.

Chancellor.

Argyle.

Hamilton.

Ruglen.

Colonel Patrick Ogilvy.

No such peer.

Stirrup cup.

B. Drafting the Treaty (1706)

Source.—*Memoirs of the Life of Sir John Clerk of Penicuik, Baronet, Baron of the Exchequer: extracted by himself from his own Journals, 1676-1755*, p. 55. (Edinburgh: Scottish Historical Society, 1892.)

We of the Committee of Parliament for the publick accompts continued our applications to the matters remitted to us till the Parliament met in September 1705. John, Duke of Argyle, a youth of about 23 years of age, was appointed her Majesty's High Commissioner, and in this station behaved himself in a manner far above what cou'd be expected from one of his years.... A ... great benefit I received by my intimacy with the Duke and his brother was to be recommended to the Queen for one of the Commissioners to be appointed by Her Majesty for the Treaty of Union between England and Scotland.... This choise, however honourable to me, was very far from giving me the least pleasure or satisfaction, for I had observed a great backwardness in the Parliament of Scotland for an Union with England of any kind whatsoever, and therefore doubted not but, after a great deal of expense in attending a Treaty in England, I should be oblidged to return with the uneasy reflexion of having either done nothing, or nothing to the purpose, as had been the case of former Commissioners appointed for this end. I was, in short, upon the point of refusing the Honour conferred upon me, and the rather that my Father, whom I always considered as an Oracle seldom mistaken, seemed not to approve of it. However, as at last he grew passive, and that the Duke of Queensberry threatened to withdraw all friendship for me, I suffered my self to be prevailed upon, and to take journey for London with other Commissioners, and arrived there on the 13 of Aprile 1706.

... The Commissioners of both nations met in different apartments in the Royal palace of Westminster, which commonly goes under the name of the Cockpit. There was one great Room where they all met when they were called upon to attend the Queen, or were to exchange papers, but they never met to hold conferences together except once, when the number of the Scotch Representatives for the two Houses of the British Parliament came to be debated, all their transactions were reduced in writings concerted in seperat apartments. When proposals or Conditions of the Union were to be made by the English Commissioners, the Scots were desired to meet them in the great Room, and their proposals were given in by the Ld Chancellor, or the Keeper of the great seal, who was at that time the Lord Cooper, and when the Commissioners for Scotland had any thing to propose, or had answers to be made to the Commissioners of England, these were presented by the Ld Seafield, then Chancellor for Scotland....

The first grand point debated by the Commissioners for Scotland amongst themselves was whether they should propose to the English a Federal union between the two nations, or an Incorporating union. The first was most favoured by the people of Scotland, but all the Scots Commissioners, to a Man, considered it ridiculous and impracticable, for that in all the Federal unions there behoved to be a supreme power lodged somewhere, and wherever this was lodged it henceforth became the States General, or, in our way of speaking, the Parliament of Great Britain, under the same royal power and authority as the two nations are at present. And in things of the greatest consequence to the two nations, as in Councils relating to peace and war and subsidies, it was impossible that the Representatives or their suffrages in both nations cou'd be equal, but must be regulated in proportion to the power and riches of the several publick burdens or Taxations that cou'd affect them; in a word, the Scots Commissioners saw that no Union cou'd subsist between the two nations but an incorporating perpetual one. But after all the trouble we gave ourselves to please the people of Scotland, we knew at the time that it was but losing our labour, for the English Commissioners were positively resolved to treat on no kind of union with us but what was to be incorporating and perpetual....

The Queen came among us three several times, once at our first or second meeting, to acquaint us of her intentions and ardent good wishes for our success and unanimity in this great Transaction. At about a month thereafter she came again to enquire of our success, and had most of our Minutes read to her, and for the last time of what we had done....

I was ... intrusted with another province by the Commissioners for Scotland, which was to review the Calculations made for the Equivalent to be paid to Scotland for bearing their share of the Debt of England, which were afterwards to be considered as the Debts of Great Britain. These calculations were chiefly made by Doctor Gregory, professor of Mathematicks in the College of Oxford, and a certain great accomptant and projector, one Patersone, from Scotland, but bred in England from his infancy....

One day I had occasion to observe the Calamities which attend human nature even in the greatest dignities of Life. Her majesty was labouring under a fit of the Gout, and in extream pain and agony, and on this occasion every thing about her was much in the same disorder as about the meanest of her subjects. Her face, which was red and spotted, was rendered something frightful by her negligent dress, and the foot affected was tied up with a pultis and some nasty bandages. I was much affected at this sight, and the more *when she had occasion to mention her people of Scotland*, which she did frequently to the Duke. What are you, poor meanlike Mortal, thought I, who talks in the style of a Soveraign? Nature seems to be inverted when a poor infirm Woman becomes one of the Rulers of the World, but, as Tacitus observes, it is not the first time that Women have governed in Britain, and indeed they have sometimes done this to better purpose than the Men.

But to return to the Treaty of Union, the Articles were at last agreed to, sign'd, and sealed, by all the Commissioners, the 22 of July 1706. They were afterwards presented to the Queen at her palace of St James, before a very numerous Assembley.

FOOTNOTES:

Founder of the Bank of England, and originator of the Darien Scheme.

C. Popular Hostility To the Union (1706)

Source.—*The History of the Union of Great Britain*, part iv., p. 27, by Daniel De Foe. (Edinburgh: 1709).

The common people now screw'd up to a pitch, and ripe for the mischief designed, and prompted by the particular agents of a wicked party, began to be very insolent: It had been whispered about several days, that the rabble would rise, and come up to the Parliament House; and cry No Union; that they would take away the Honours, as they call them, viz. the Crown etc., and carry them to the Castle, and a long variety of foolish reports of this kind. But the first appearance of anything mobish was, that every day, when the Duke went up, but principally as he came down in his chair from the House, the mob follow'd him, shouting and crying out, GOD bless his Grace, for standing up against the Union, and appearing for his country, and the like.... On the 22nd of October, they follow'd the Duke's chair quite thro the city down to the Abbey Gate; the guards prevented their going further; but all the way as they came back, they were heard to threaten what they would do the next day; that then they would be a thousand times as many; that they would pull the traitors, so they called the treaters of the Union at London, out of their houses, and they would soon put an end to the Union.

On the 23rd they made part of their words good indeed; for, as the Parliament sat something late, the people gather'd in the streets, and about the doors of the Parliament House, and particularly the Parliament Close was almost full, that the members could not go in or out without difficulty; when Duke Hamilton was coming out of the House, the mob huzza'd as formerly, and follow'd his chair in a very great number; the Duke, instead of going down to the Abbey as usual, went up the High Street to the Land-Market, as they call it, and so to the lodgings of the Duke of Athole; some said, he went to avoid the mob; others maliciously said, he went to point them to their work.

While he went in to the Duke of Athole's lodgings, the rabble attended at the door; and, by shouting and noise, having increased their numbers to several thousands, they began with Sir Patrick Johnston, who was one of the treaters, and the year before had been Lord Provost; first they assaulted his lodgings with stones and sticks, and curses not a few; but his windows being too high, they came up the stairs to his door, and fell to work at it with sledges, or great hammers; and, had they broke it open in their first fury, he had, without doubt, been torn in pieces without mercy; and thus only, because he was a treater in the commission to England; for, before that, no man was so well belov'd, as he, over the whole city.

His lady, in the utmost despair with this fright, comes to the window, with two candles in her hand, that she might be known; and cried out, for GOD'S sake, to call the guards; an honest apothecary in the town, who knew her voice, and saw the distress she was in, and to whom the family, under GOD, is obliged, for their deliverance, ran immediately down to the town guard; but they would not stir, without the Lord Provost's order; but that being soon obtain'd, one Captain Richardson, who commanded, taking about thirty men with him, march'd bravely up to them; and making his way with great resolution thro the crowd, they flying, but throwing stones, and hallowing at him, and his men, he seized the foot of the stair case; and then boldly went up, clear'd the stair, and took six of the rabble in the very act; and so delivered the gentleman and his family....

The city was now in a terrible fright, and every body was under concern for their friends; the rabble went raving about the streets till midnight, frequently beating drums, and raising more people; when my Lord Commissioner being informed, there were a thousand of the seamen and rabble come up from Leith; and apprehending, if it were suffered to go on, it might come to a dangerous head, and be out of his power to suppress, he sent for the Lord Provost, and demanded, that the Guards should march into the city.

The Lord Provost, after some difficulty, yielded; tho it was alleged, that it was what was never known in Edinburgh before. About one o clock in the morning, a battalion of the Guards entered the town, marched up to the Parliament Close, and took post in all the avenues of the city, which prevented the resolutions taken to insult the houses of the rest of the treaters.

The rabble were intirely reduc'd by this, and gradually dispers'd, and so the tumult ended....

The author of this had his share in the danger of this tumult, and tho unknown to him, was watch'd and set by the mob, in order to know where to find him, had his chamber windows insulted, and the windows below him broken by mistake. But, by the prudence of his friends, the shortness of its continuance, and GOD'S providence, he escaped.

FOOTNOTES:

Of Hamilton. An opponent of the Union.

The Lawn Market.

De Foe was known to be staying in Edinburgh as the emissary of the English Government.

D. "An End of an Old Song" (1707)

Source.—*The Lockhart Papers: containing Memoirs and Commentaries upon the Affairs of Scotland from* 1702 *to* 1715, vol. i., p. 222, by George Lockhart, Esq., of Carnwath. (London: 1817.)

It is not to be doubted, but the Parliament of England would give a kind reception to the articles of the Union as passed in Scotland, when they were laid before that House, as was evident from the quick dispatch in approving of and ratifying the same; and so the Union commenced on the first of May 1707, a day never to be forgot by Scotland; a day in which the Scots were stripped of what their predecessors had gallantly maintained for many hundred years, I mean the independency and soveraignty of the kingdom, both which the Earl of Seafield so little valued, that when he, as Chancellor, signed the engrossed exemplification of the Act of Union, he returned it to the clerk, in the face of Parliament, with this dispising and contemning remark, "Now there's ane end of ane old song."

"THE WEE, WEE GERMAN LAIRDIE" (1714)

Source.—*The Jacobite Songs and Ballads of Scotland from 1688 to 1746*, p. 65. Edited by Charles Mackay, LL.D. (London and Glasgow: 1861.)

Wha the deil hae we gotten for a King,But a wee, wee German lairdie!An' when we gaed to bring him hame,He was delving in his kail-yairdie:Sheughing kail, and laying leeks,But the hose and but the breeks;Up his beggar duds he cleeks,The wee, wee German lairdie!

And he's clapt down in our gudeman's chair,The wee, wee German lairdie!And he's brought fouth o' foreign trash,And dibbled them in his yairdie:He's pu'd the rose o' English loons,And brake the harp o' Irish clowns,But our Scots thristle will jag his thumbs,The wee, wee German lairdie.

Come up among the Highland hills,Thou wee, wee German lairdie.And see how Charlie's lang-kail thrive,That he dibbled in his yairdie:And if a stock ye daur to pu',Or haud the yoking of a pleugh,We'll break your sceptre o'er your mou',Thou wee bit German lairdie!

Our hills are steep, our glens are deep,No fitting for a yairdie;And our norlan' thristles winna pu',Thou wee, wee German lairdie! And we've the trenching blades o' weir,Wad lib ye o' your German gear,And pass ye 'neath the claymore's shear,Thou feckless German lairdie!

He'll ride nae mair on strae sonks,For gawing his German hurdies;But he sits on our gude king's throne,Amang the English lordies.Auld Scotland! thou'rt owre cauld a holeFor nursing siccan vermin;But the very dogs o' England's courtCan bark and howl in *German*!

FOOTNOTES:

Written on the accession of King George I.

Literally, vegetable garden.

Trenching.

Colewort.

Outside.

Shabby clothes.

Grabs.

Abundance.

Planted.

Lacerate.

Unmashed cabbage.

Mouth.

Northland.

War.

Geld.

Incompetent.

Loose straw rubbish.

Chafing.

Buttocks.

Suchlike.

THE RISING OF 1715
A. GATHERING OF THE CLANS (SEPTEMBER)

Source.—*The History of the Rebellion rais'd against His Majesty King George I. by the Friends of the Popish Pretender*, p. 187, by the Reverend Mr. Peter Rae. Second edition. (London: 1746.)

The Earl of Mar, then at London, not finding how to form his own interest at court, had resolved on those wicked and traitorous measures he afterwards followed; and in order to raise and carry on the rebellion, had, by some means or other, received from abroad, no less than the sum of one hundred thousand pounds sterling, together with letters and instructions under the Pretender's own hand, and a commission appointing him Lieutenant-General and Commander in Chief of his forces, as he called them, in Scotland: And fearing lest his traitorous designs against his lawful sovereign prince, to whom he had so early and solemnly promised fidelity, might possibly be discovered, and he himself secured by the government, he resolved to make a sudden tour into Scotland, as the likeliest mean to prevent this fate, and in order to make some speedy advances in this his pernicious and bloody undertaking. Wherefore on the 2nd of August, or as some say, the 1st, in the evening, his lordship, in the dress of a private person, embark'd with Major-General Hamilton, Colonel Hay, and two servants on board of a collier in the Thames, and arriving in two or three days at Newcastle, hired there a vessel belonging to one Spence, which set him and his company on shore in the Ely, from whence he got over to Creil in the shire of Fife. Soon after his landing he was attended by Sir Alexander Areskine, Lord Lyon, and others of his friends in Fife, to whom he made known the design of his coming, and then went forward to Kinoul, where he staid on Wednesday the 17th, and on the 18th he passed the river Tay, about two miles from Perth, with 40 horse on his way to the north. Next day he sent letters to all the Jacobites round the country, inviting them to meet him in haste at Brae-Mar, where he arrived on Saturday the 20th of August.

There is no room to doubt, that he had before-hand concerted measures with them; and that they were previously advised of his coming, before he arrived in Scotland: For, on Saturday the 6th of August, their friends at Edinburgh were apprized of it; and early next morning Captain John Dalziel, a half-pay officer, who, in view of this rebellion had thrown up his commission to the Earl of Orkney, was sent out to give the alarm to his brother, the Earl of Carnwath, then at Elliock, where he arrived that night; and, early next morning, expresses were sent to the Earl of Nithsdale, the Viscount of Kenmure, and others of their friends in those parts; the Earl himself went down that same day to meet them, in order to forward their measures; and after some time spent in preparing others, whose inclinations they knew, to embark with them in that bloody project, they repaired to Lothian; and 'twas then given out, that they were gone to a hunting in the north. This was indeed a plausible pretence for their getting to the Highlands, and the more that the Earl of Mar, to cover his design, too black to be owned at the first, in calling the chiefs of the clans together, had proposed a hunting in his own country. Accordingly, in a few days after he arrived at Brae-Mar, he was there attended by a great number of gentlemen, of the best quality and interest of all his party: And particularly at their Great Council, which was held about August 26, there appeared the Marquis of Huntley, eldest son to the Duke of Gordon; the Marquis of Tullibardine, eldest son to the Duke of Athol; the Earls of Nithsdale, Marischal, Traquair, Errol, Southesk, Carnwath, Seaforth, Linlithgow, and several others; the Viscounts of Kilsith, Kenmure, Kingston and Stormount; the Lords Rollo, Duffus, Drummond, Strathallan, Ogilvie and Nairn, with a good many gentlemen of interest in the Highlands, amongst whom were the two Generals, Hamilton and Gordon, Glenderule, Auldbair, Auchterhouse, Glengary, and others from the clans....

... Moreover, we are told, that he shew'd them the letters he had received from Lorraine, under the Pretender's own hand, promising to come over to them in person, and put himself upon the valour and fidelity of his Scots subjects; and that in the mean time, they should be sure of ships, with arms, ammunition, and all military stores, with officers, engineers, and volunteers, as soon as they could give him an account to what port they would direct them to be sent: As also, that he shew'd them his commission under the Pretender's own hand, appointing him Lieutenant-General, Commander in Chief, and Director of the War; and assur'd them, that he was furnish'd with money, and would, from time to time, be supplied with sufficient sums to levy men, and to pay the troops regularly that should be raised; so as no gentlemen should be at any expence to subsist their men, but that both they, and the country should be eased of all such burthens.

With these and other such arguments, which he proposed unto them with a popular air, he at length prevailed upon them to embrace his project; and some say, they engaged by oath to stand by him, and one another, and to bring over their friends and dependants to do the like. However, the noblemen and gentlemen did not immediately after this meeting draw together their men, but went every man back to his own estate, to take their measures for appearing in arms, when they should hear again from the Earl of Mar, who remain'd, in the mean time, in his own country, with some few attendants only. These noblemen and gentlemen being returned home, began to draw together their servants and dependants, in all the places where they had interest, making several pretences for doing so, but did not discover the real design till things were in readiness to break out. And indeed it was but a few days after, that the Earl of Mar summon'd them all, at least such as were near at hand, to a general meeting at Aboyne in Aberdeenshire, on the third of September, in order to concert farther measures for their appearing in arms: And having there directed the drawing together their forces without any loss of time, he returned to Brae-Mar, and continued some days gathering the people, till their number was increased considerably; but the accounts being so various, while some say there were then two thousand men, most of them horse, and others but sixty, I shall not condescend on the particular number: However, with those he had got together, he set up the Pretender's Standard at Brae-Mar, on the sixth of September, 1715, and there proclaim'd him King of Scotland, England, France, and Ireland, etc. 'Tis reported, that when this standard was first erected, the ball on the top of it fell off, which the superstitious Highlanders were very much concern'd at, taking it as an omen of the bad success of the cause for which they were then appearing, and indeed, the event has proven that it was no less. Thereafter they went to a small town named Kirkmichael, where having proclaim'd the Pretender, and summon'd the people to attend his standard, they staid some few days, and then proceeded to Moulin, another small town in the shire of Perth, where they likewise proclaim'd him, and rested some short time, gathering their forces; and where by the coming in of others of their party, their number was considerably increased.

FOOTNOTES:

George I.

Crail.

B. DEFENCE OF EDINBURGH (OCTOBER)

Source.—*Memoirs of the Life of Sir John Clerk of Penicuik, Bart.: extracted by himself from his own Journals, 1676-1755*, p. 89. Edited by John M. Gray. (Edinburgh: Scottish Historical Society, 1892.)

In the mean time it must be confessed that their courage and conduct in Scotland far exceeded what was expected, for the Earl of Mar had so much address as to bring to the town of Perth, the center of all the enterprise, at least 10,000 men, some have carried the number to 12,000, which *I* am inclined to believe, provided the 1600 men be included that past the Frith of Forth near the Island of May, of which hereafter.

During these convulsions in my native country, I was obliged to change my course of living and turn a military man, for being appointed one of the Lieutenants of the Shire of Edin., I was obliged to act my part in bringing the militia together. These consisted of a few men, horse and foot, who never continued 3 days together, and signified nothing in the military way, the lowland men being a great deal more unfit for warlike expeditions than the Highlanders who had joined the Earl of Mar. However, with these militia troops we sometimes made a show, and perhaps they served to intimidate those who knew nothing about them. They were particularly useful and active when the Highlanders above mentioned past the Forth and were marching to take possession of Edin., for being drawn up on the high way a mile east of Edin., where these Highlanders were to march in order to take possession of the town, they found themselves obliged to turn to the right and take possession of the citadel of Lieth, the —— of October, 1715.

That same night, to the joy of the inhabitants of Edin., who expected to be plundered by the Highlanders, the Duke of Argyll arrived from Stirling with 200 chosen foot and 300 dragoons, the foot mounted on country horses for more expedition. Next morning the Deputy Lieutenants and all the well affected to the Government of K. George waited on him, and immediately he ordered all his troops to march down with him to the attaque of the Citadel of Lieth.

I waited on his Grace, and we never halted till we were within 300 paces of that place. Here all our men were drawn up in 2 lines for the attaque. The foot in the center, and the horse on the wings, our number was as follows. 300 Dragoons, 200 Regular foot, about 200 of the Town Guards of Edin., and about 500 volunteers, with a regiment of militia. These amounting in all to about 1500 men, were drawn up on the crofts to the westward of the citadel. There were likeways two regiments of militia from the shires of Merse and Teviotdale, who were drawn up on the Links on the south side of the town to prevent the Highlanders from escaping.

The Duke called a Council of War, consisting of the principal officers present, in sight of the enemy, here it was debated in what manner to attaque the citadel, for the duke had never seen it, and the issue was that in regard we had neither cannon, bombs, nor granads, it was impossible to do anything to purpose, for that our men would be destroied by the fire of the enemy before they came near the ramparts, for altho' these ramparts and bastions were ruined ever since the days of Oliver Cromwell, who about the years 1654 and 1655 ordered them to be repaired out of the old fortifications of Lieth, yet they were sufficient against such a body of men as we were who came there to attaque them. On these considerations we were obliged to return to the town in a very disconsolet manner.

The Duke might have been informed of the condition of that place before he marched there, but he thought nothing in Scotland, except castles, impregnable to his troops, and we who knew the citadel never doubted but dismounted Dragoons cou'd force the place sword in hand. The next thing to be done was to provide artillery from the Castle of Edin., in order to attaque the citadel next day, but that night the Highlanders, who were under the command of one Brigadier Macintosh, marched off to Seaton House, where they staid 3 or 4 days. Here several detachments were sent out of Edin. to attaque them, but being without cannon we cou'd do nothing.

FOOTNOTES:

14th.

C. The Battle of Sheriffmuir (November)

Source.—*A Fragment of a Memoir of Field-Marshal James Keith: written by himself, 1714-1734*, p. 16. (Edinburgh: Spalding Club, 1843.)

All our troops being now assembled, the Earl of Mar resolved to march towards the enemy, and on the eighth of November arrived at Denain, with fourteen battalions of foot and eight squadrons of horse, having left three battalions in Perth for the defence of the place; the ninth the army lay at Auchterarder, where he reviewed the troops, who consisted of about 6000 foot and eight hundred horse. Here we lay two days, waiting for two battalions from Fife; but finding these did not come up so soon as we expected, the twelfth we continued our march, the advanced guard lay near Dumblain, and the rest of the troops were quarter'd about a mile behind them, the want of tents and the coldness of the weather rendering it impossible for us to encamp. We had as yet no perfect account of the motions of the enemy, and concluded from the inferiority of their number (they being not above 3000 foot and twelve hundred horse), that they would fight us at the passage of the river, but we had hardly got the troops marched to their different quarters, when we received orders to join with all haste our advanced guard, the Duke of Argile having passed the Forth, and encamped about the toun of Dumblain, within cannon shot of them. Both armies lay all night on their arms, and next morning by day break we discover'd a body of the enemies on a rising ground near our left. Before eight in the morning, our army was formed in order of battle, in two lines, without any body of reserve. The Earl of Mar call'd all the general officers and heads of clans to a council of war, which was held at the head of the line, and there asked their advice whither we should attack the enemy, or return to Perth and wait the arrival of King James, who was every day expected, as also for accounts what success our friends in England might have; but it was carried almost unanimously to attack, none daring openly to oppose the current; the Marquis of Huntly only made some insinuations that it would not be fit to remain in unaction till the King's arrival.

The resolution being now taken to attack the enemy, the Earl of Mar commanded the Earl Marischal, with Sir Donald M'Donald's regiment of foot, and his own squadron of horse, to take possession of the rising ground on which a body of the enemies horse still remain'd, and to cover the march of the army on the left (our right being cover'd by a river) to the toun of Dumblain, where we imagined the enemy still to be. On our approach, the enemies horse retired; and we had no sooner gained the top of the hill than we discover'd their whole body, marching without beat of drum, about two musket shot from us. It was now too late to retreat; we therfor form'd on the top of the hill, and the Earl Marischal sent an aid-de-camp to advertise the Earl of Mar that he was fallen in with the enemies army, that it was impossible for him to bring off the foot, and therfor desired he would march up to his assistance as quick as possible,—which he did even in too much haste; for the army, which marched in four columns, arrived in such confusion that it was impossible to form them according to the line of battle projected, every one posted himself as he found ground, and one column of foot enclining to the right and another to the left of the Earl Marischal's squadron of horse, that regiment which should have been on the right, found itself in the center, separated from the rest of the horse, and opposed to the enemies foot; our foot formed all in one line, except on the left, where a bog hinder'd them from extending themselves, and encreased the confusion.

The Duke of Argile was no less embarrassed on his side. His army was not yet entirely formed; the rear, which was to have formed his left wing, was yet on their march, and showed us their flanck, which being observed by Lieutenant General Gordon, he order'd our troops immediately to charge, which they did with so much vigour that in less than ten minutes they entirely defeated six regiments of foot and five squadrons of dragoons, which composed more than the half of the Duke's army, while the rest having taken the same advantage of our left, which had neither time nor ground to fire, entirely routed them. Both parties pursued the troops they had broken, not knowing what had happen'd on the other side, till at length the Earl of Mar, having had the fatal news of the loss we had receiv'd, order'd the troops to give over the pursuit, and having rallied them, returned to the field of battle, from whence we discover'd the enemy posted at the foot of the hill amongst mud walls, on the same ground where we had layen the night before.

The Earl of Mar sent immediately an officer to reconnoitre them, and at the same time assembled the General officers and heads of clans, to consult whether he should attack them again; but the officer having reported that their numbers were equal to ours, and the Highlanders, who were extreamly fatigued, and had eat nothing in two days, being averse to it, it was resolved to keep the field of battle, and to let the enemy retire unmolested, which they had already began to do under cover of the earth walls, as well as of the night which was now approaching, leaving us about fifty prisoners of ours, most of them wounded, whom they had not time to carry along with them. We continued on the field of battle till dark night, and then marched back to the same villages which had been marked for our quarters the night before.

The enemy had about seven hundred men killed or wounded, amongst whom was the Earl of Forfar killed, and the Earl of Islay wounded, and two hundred and twenty-three taken prisoners, and we had about 150 killed or wounded, and eighty-two taken; but among those killed we had three persons of note, the Earl of Strathmore, his unkle Auchterhouse, and Clanronald, and the Earl of Panmure very much wounded. The loss of colours was almost equal on both sides; but the enemy got five piece of our cannon, which we could not carry off, those belonging to the train having run away with the horses when they saw our left broke; and thus ended the affair of Dumblain, in which neither side gained much honour, but which was the entire ruin of our party.

Some unlucky mistakes which happened that day, must here take place; first, an order to the whole horse on the left to march to the right, which so discouraged the foot of that wing to see themselves abandoned, that to it may be attributed their shameful behaviour that day; nor were these horse of any advantage to us where they were posted, for the ground was so bad that they could never be brought to engage. Another, of no less consequence, was the mistake of the officer who was sent to reconnoitre the Duke of Argile's army in the afternoon, for he having taken his remarks more by the number of colours than the space of ground they occupied, made his report that the enemy was betwixt two and three thousand foot strong, when in reality there was no more than three battalions, not making in all above one thousand foot, the other colours being what the Duke had just taken on our left, and being almost the same with his own, he now used them to disguise the weakness of his troops by making a show of four battalions more than he had, the ground and mud walls by which he was cover'd not allowing to see that he had formed only two ranks deep; this mistake hinder'd us from attacking him in the evening, which it's probable we might have done with better success than we had in the morning.

Next morning the Duke of Mar, finding most of our left had run quite away and was not yet returned, retired towards Perth, as the enemy had already done into Stirling.

FOOTNOTES:

Dunning, in Perthshire.

D. THE OLD PRETENDER (DECEMBER)

Source.—*Memoirs of the Insurrection in Scotland in 1715, by John, Master of Sinclair*, p. 333. Edited from the original manuscript by Sir Walter Scott, Bart. (Edinburgh: Abbotsford Club, 1848.)

Before these had come to Huntlie, the King was already landed at Peterhead, the twenty-seventh day of September [December], and was in his road to Fetteresso, where he halted. We were not long of hearing from those who came from the South that a young gentleman had passed Aberdeen with Captain Allan Cameron; that they had gone straight to Fetteresso, and it was thought that young man was the King; Cameron was gone on post to Perth, and the other was left at Fetteresso privately. This made Huntlie send a gentleman to Aberdeen with orders to go on till he got the certain account. By the time he got there, he was certainly informed the King was arrived, and that Mar was already at Fetteresso. To do Huntlie justice, being present when he received the news, he said, "Now ther's no help for it, we must all ruin with him: would to God he had comed sooner." There seem'd still some faint hopes to remain, which were, that since his Majestie had stopt at Fetteresso, and kept himself incognito there for two days, till Captain Cameron had informed Mar of his arrival, his reason for it could only be that he wanted to know the state of his affairs before he'd go forward to Perth; for what other reason could have hinder'd him to [have] declared himself at Aberdeen, or from going straight to Perth? And by all that could be learned since, we found we judged right; for it's said, that if his affairs were on a bad foot, he was resolved to return without loss of time, and leave his poor subjects the freedom of making terms for themselves; a very just and reasonable thought. Whatever was in it, as his declaring himself at Fetteresso, and afterwards going up to Perth, put a stop to all thoughts of terms on our side, so it's not to be doubted that the Government, however inclinable they might [have] been before, could ever entertain or allow of any such proposals from those inclined to mercy, or the moderate people of their own side....

My Lord Mar, who, as we first supposed, would [have] met his Majesty privately, spread the news at Perth of the King's happy landing, and brought a numerous train with him to Fetteresso, out of a view, I believe, to put it out of his Majesty's power to go back, having already published his being there; and to confirm him of the certainty of his affairs succeeding, by the approbation of those villainous, weak, miserable, deluded dependers of his Lordship, who he brought along with him.

... Thus that unhappy Prince, entirely a stranger to his own affairs, as much as he had dropt out of another world, or from the clouds, as things stood, was brought in eminent danger of his life, without its being possible that it could have any other effect but that of the certain ruin of his friends, and driving the nail to the head, and riveting the misery of those who had so generously sacrificed all to serve him. It's certain that he was made believe that his affairs in general were on a good foot, at least, very retrievable; that there were twice as many in Perth as there really were; and that there was no more needful to be done but the taking of Inverness, which entirely depended on Huntlie; and when that was done, the King would have a great army from all places of the Highlands before the Duke of Argyle could attack Perth. As for powder, I suppose it was never spoke of, since there was no want of it at Fetteresso; that the news of his Majestie's arrival would no sooner spread but all would return, and great numbers who had joined them would come from different corners.... The King was carried triumphinglie up to Perth.

FOOTNOTES:

The Marquis of Huntly.

It should be the 22nd of December.

E. COLLAPSE OF THE REBELLION (1716)

Source.—*The History of the Rebellion rais'd against His Majesty King George I. by the Friends of the Popish Pretender*, p. 365, by the Rev. Mr. Peter Rae. Second edition. (London: 1746.)

... His Grace having received positive orders from Court, to march forthwith against the rebels, he resolved to surmount all difficulties, and to march as soon as the artillery, and some of the Dutch forces at Edinburgh, and the regiments of Newton and Stanhope, who were quartered at Glasgow, could come up to join him; which they did, two or three days after.... The news of these preparations and march were not grateful to His Majesty at Scone, spoiling the ceremony of his coronation, and meeting of his Parliament: Instead of which fine things, the only matter now under consideration was, how to provide for their own safety; and the grand question debated was, whether to maintain the place, and fight the Duke of Argyle, or retreat.... The Pretender, finding that time was not to be lost, retired that evening from Scone to Perth, where having supped at Provost Hay's, he rested some hours; and next morning about ten o'clock, the rebels abandoned Perth, marching over the Tay upon the ice, and, leaving their cannon behind them, took their rout towards Dundee. About noon the Pretender himself, with the Earl of Mar, followed his flying adherents with tears in his eyes, complaining that instead of bringing him to a Crown, they had brought him to his grave....

The rebels having retired from Dundee to Montrose, his Grace, on the 3rd, sent a detachment towards Aberbrothick within eight miles of that place; and on the fourth, in the morning, ordered Major General Sabine, with 3 battalions, 500 detached foot, and 50 dragoons, to march to Aberbrothick. The same day his Grace detached Colonel Clayton with 300 foot and 50 dragoons, to march by the way of Brechin; giving orders to the one as well as the other to summon the country people to remove the snow on the roads, which, being then very deep, made their march very heavy and tedious. His Grace having divided the rest of his army into two bodies, for marching with the greater expedition; and the rebel army having marched in two columns, on the 5th, in the morning, General Cadogan with the infantry marched towards Aberbrothick, and at the same time the Duke himself, with all the cavalry, proceeded by the Upper Road towards Brechin; the whole army being to join the next day at Stonehive, intending on Tuesday hereafter to be at Aberdeen, to which place they supposed the Pretender was gone.

But by this time the Pretender was out of their reach; for having received advice at Montrose, on the 4th of February, about four in the afternoon, that part of the King's army was advancing towards Aberbrothick, he ordered the clans who remained with him to be ready to march, about eight at night, towards Aberdeen, where he assured them a considerable force would soon come to them from France. At the hour appointed for their march, the Pretender ordered his horses to be brought before the door of the house in which he lodged, and the guard which usually attended him to mount, as if he designed to go on with the clans to Aberdeen; but at the same time he slipped privately out on foot, accompanied only by one of his domesticks, went to the Earl of Mar's lodgings, and from thence, by a byway to the water-side, where a boat waited and carried him and the Earl of Mar on board a French ship of 90 tuns, called the *Maria Teresa* of St. Malo. About a quarter of an hour after, two other boats carried the Earl of Melford and the Lord Drummond, with Lieutenant-General Sheldon and ten other gentlemen on board the same ship, and then they hoisted sail and put to sea; and notwithstanding of his Majesty's ships that were cruising on that coast, got safely off, and in seven days landed at Waldam, near Graveling, between Dunkirk and Calais. The Earls Marischal, Southesk, the Lord Tinmouth, General Gordon, with many other gentlemen and officers of distinction, were left behind to shift for themselves, who kept with the army, and continued their march towards Aberdeen, the foot marching on before with General Gordon, and the Earl Marischal, with about 1000 horse, keeping the rear to prevent surprise....

The same day the King's forces advanced to Montrose, the remains of the rebel army arrived at Aberdeen, where General Gordon showed them a letter from the Pretender, in which he acquainted his friends that the disappointments he had met with, especially from abroad, had obliged him to leave that country; that he thanked them for their services, and desired them to advise with General Gordon, and consult their own security either by keeping in a body or separating, and encouraging them to expect to hear farther from him in a very short time.... And we are told, that upon reading of the letter, many of the people threw down their arms, crying out they were basely betrayed, they were all undone, they were left without king or general. On the seventh, in the morning, the van of the rebels marched from Aberdeen, as did their rear about two in the afternoon, and their main body lay at Old Meldrum that night; but about 200 of their horse, amongst whom were many of their chiefs, with Irish and other officers who came lately from France, went toward Peterhead in order to ship themselves off in ships which they knew were waiting for them there....

Their main body marched straight west, through Strath-Spey and Strath-Don to the hills of Badenoch, where they separated: The foot dispersed into the mountains on this side of Lochy, and the horse went Lochquhaher, agreeing, however, to meet again upon notice from the Pretender. And here being advised that two French frigates were come for their relief, and would lay in Pentland Firth till they should hear from them, the Lord Duffus, Sir George Sinclair, General Eckline and others, about 160 gentlemen in all, well mounted on horseback, made a sally from the hills, and crossing the shire of Murray, came to the seaside near Burgh, where they got several large barks which carried them to the Orkneys, Arskerry, and other of the islands, from whence most of them found means to get into the frigates which carried them safe to France. Other ships coming afterwards carried the rest to Gottenburg, in the Swedish dominions, where some of them took on in that king's service.... There were yet with the rebels in Scotland many of their chiefs, as the Marquis of Tullibardine, the Earls Marischal, Southesk, Linlithgow, and Seaforth, who having broke his submission, joined them again in their flight to the northward, the Lord Tinmouth, Sir Donald M'Donald, and several others of the heads of the clans, who sheltered themselves for some time in the mountains from his Majesty's troops who pursued them through the north; and from thence some made their escape to the Isle of Sky, the Lewis, and other of the north-western islands till ships came for their relief to carry them abroad; and some of them afterwards submitted to the Government, as we shall hear below....

The Duke of Argyle having thus gloriously finished the most laborious and hard campaign that ever was known, he left the command of his Majesty's troops to Lieutenant-General Cadogan and returned to Edinbourgh the 27th of February, and in a day or two after set out for London, where he arrived on the 6th of March.

FOOTNOTES:

Of Argyle.

January 30.

Of February.

Arbroath.

Stonehaven.

Gravelines.

Moray.

Eriska.

F. Harshness of the Government (1716)

Source.—*Culloden Papers: comprising an Extensive and Interesting Correspondence from the Year 1625 to 1678 ... the Whole published from the Originals in the Possession of Duncan George Forbes, of Culloden, Esq.*, p. 61. (London: 1815.)

No. LXXII.

An anonymous letter, written by Mr. Duncan Forbes to Sir Robert Walpole, most likely in August 1716—a copy is extant (from which the present is taken) in the President's handwriting.

Sir, ... When the late Rebellion was happily ended by the Pretender's flight, his deluded followers found themselves all in chains, or obliged to surrender and sue for mercy, or to fly their country with him. Every man concerned in that odious work certainly deserved death, and the punishment due by law; but humanity and prudence forbade it. It was not fit to dispeople a country; nor prudent to grieve the King's best friends, who mostly had some concern in those unfortunate men; or expedient to give too just grounds of clamour to the disaffected.

It will be agreed on all hands, that the proper rule in this case would have been, to have punished only as many as was necessary for terror, and for weakening the strength of the rebels for the future; and to extend mercy to as many as it could conveniently be indulged to with the security of the Government; and this maxim every thinking Whig had then in his mouth, however offended at the insolences of the rebels. In place of a course of this kind, the method followed was, 1st, to try all the criminals in England; 2dly, to detain in prison all those in custody in Scotland, except some who had interest with certain great men to obtain a previous pardon, to the manifest dishonour of the Government; 3dly, to attaint a vast number of Scots noblemen and gentlemen; 4thly, to put it out of his Majesty's power to grant any part of estates forfeited; and 5thly, to appoint a Commission for enquiry, and levying the rebels' goods and chattels. The necessary consequences of this procedure in general are two; first, it makes all those who had the misfortune to be seduced into the rebellion, with their children, relatives, and such as depend on them, forever desperate; and it's hard to tell what occasions may offer for venting their rage. We see that want and hard circumstances lead men daily into follies, without any other temptation; but when those circumstances are brought on by adherence to any principle, or opinion, it's certain the sufferers will not quit their attempts to better their condition, but with their lives. 2d, as there are none of the rebels who have not friends among the King's faithful subjects, it is not easy to guess how far a severity of this kind, unnecessarily pushed, may alienate the affections even of those from the Government. But in particular, as this case relates to Scotland, the difficulty will be insurmountable. I may venture to say, there are not 200 gentlemen in the whole kingdom who are not very nearly related to some one or other of the rebels. Is it possible that a man can see his daughter, his grandchildren, his nephews, or cousins, reduced to beggary and starving unnecessarily by a Government, without thinking very ill of it; and where this is the case of a whole nation, I tremble to think what dissatisfactions it will produce against a settlement so necessary for the happiness of Britain.

If all the rebels, with their wives, children, and immediate dependants, could be at once rooted out of the earth, the shock would be astonishing; but time would commit it to oblivion, and the danger would be less to the Constitution, than when thousands of innocents, punished with misery and want for the offences of their friends, are suffered to wander about the country, sighing out their complaints to Heaven, and drawing at once the compassion and moving the indignation of every human creature.

THE SCOTTISH CAPITAL

Source.—*A Journey through Scotland, in Familiar Letters from a Gentleman here, to his Friend Abroad*, p. 65, by J. Macky. Second edition. (London: 1729.)

The High-Street of Edinburgh, running by an easy ascent from the Netherbow to the Castle, a good half mile, is doubtless the stateliest street in the world, being broad enough for five coaches to drive up abreast; and the houses on each side are proportionately high to the broadness of the street; all of them six or seven story high, and those mostly of free stone, makes this street very august.

Half way up this street stands St. Giles's Church, the ancient cathedral of this city, in the form of a cross; but since the Reformation it is turned into four convenient churches, by partitions, called the High-Kirk, the Old-Kirk, the Tolbooth-Kirk, and Haddock's Hole. A-top of this church is erected a large open cupola, in the shape of an imperial crown, that is a great ornament to the city, and seen at a great distance. King David erected a copy after this over St. Nicholas's Church in Newcastle, but it does not near come up to it. Besides these four churches of St. Giles's, there is in the same street a little lower the Trone Church, built after the model of Inigo Jones's St. Paul's Covent Garden; a very handsome church at the east end of the lake, called the Collegiate Church, built by Mary of Gelder, Queen to James the Second; a church built by a Lady Yester, a handsome new church in the middle of the Canongate, and two good churches under the same roof at the Grey-Friars. There are also some chapels; but they are converted into halls for trades.

To the south of St. Giles's Church is a fine square, with an equestrian statue of King Charles the Second in the middle. In this square stands the Parliament-House, where their parliaments were kept: Also the Council and Treasury, and all other publick offices. It's a fine modern building of free-stone, finished by Charles the First in 1636. Underneath this building is kept the lawyer's library; where there is a fine collection of books, of medals, and of ancient coins, the largest of English and Scots coins I ever saw. I could not perceive that the Scots bore the lion rampant in a tressor of Flower-de-Luces on the coins, till the Stewarts.

Joining to this library is the Register, where are kept all the deeds and securities of the nation, as a common bank. Here is also a very good bank for money, whose notes go current all over the nation. There is also a fine room in this square for the meeting of the royal boroughs, adorned with pictures.

In this great street are several stone fountains of water, brought in pipes at three miles distance, disposed at convenient distances to supply the whole city with water; and on each side of this street are lanes, or wynds as they are called here, that run down to the bottom.

This made an English gentleman, that was here with the Duke of York, merrily compare it to a double wooden comb, the great street the wood in the middle, and the teeth of each side the lanes.

These lanes lead you to a street below, called the Cowgate, which runs the whole length east and west of the other, but is neither half so broad or well built. The High Street is also the best paved street I ever saw. I will not except Florence. One would think the stones inlaid; they are not half a foot square; and notwithstanding the coaches and carts, there is not the least crack in it.

South from the Cowgate lies the High-School for Latin, and in its yard is kept a fine bagnio, in a handsome neat house, built for the Company of Surgeons; and in their hall is the picture of the late Duke Hamilton, Earl Finlater in his Chancellor's robes, and of all the eminent surgeons of the town, to the number of about forty, all originals, by Sir John Medina. There is also a pretty garden before and behind the house. Directly north from this, on the other side of the Cowgate, is the Physicians Hall and garden, where they have a noble museum, founded by Sir Andrew Balfour, physician. The learned and industrious Sir Robert Sebald has very much augmented it. It contains a treasure of curiosities of art and nature, foreign and domestick, as appears by Sir Robert's account, printed in four books in 1697.

A little further to the south of the Cowgate is the University, which consists only of one college: The Magistrates of Edinburgh are governors of it; it hath a principal or warden, and four philosophy regents or professors. There is also a professor of Divinity, of Civil Law, of History, Mathematicks, and Hebrew.

In studying four years at this college you commence Master of Arts: The scholars are not in commons, and kept to strict rules as in the colleges in England, nor wear gowns; they lodge and diet in the town, as at the colleges in Holland, and are required to attend at their several classes from eight in the morning till twelve, and from two to four. I wonder how a college in a town used to so much business and diversion to take off from the study of youth, should ever produce a good scholar.

This college consists of two lower courts, and one upper one, tolerably well built; the upper court, to which you ascend by steps of stairs, is larger than the other two. On the left of that court is the library, a long spacious room, and the books neatly kept, and cloistered with doors of wire, that none can open but the keeper, more commodious than the multitude of chains used in the English libraries. The several benefactions are kept in distinct apartments, with the donor's name over them in gold letters; and over these cases of books are pictures of most of the Kings of Scotland, and of all the reformers both at home and abroad....

Joining to the College is a neat hospital for girls, with a pretty garden, and bowling-green; and a little further is the churchyard of the Grey-Friars, the burial-place of all the eminent burghers of the city; for they don't affect so much as the English to be buried in churches; that they think smells too much of the Popish stamp....

To the westward of this church-yard stands the most celebrated Hospital of George Herriot, Jeweller to James the Sixth, for the bringing up of 130 poor boys, children of decayed merchants and tradesmen of this city. The building exceeds any thing of the kind in Europe. Sutton's Hospital, called the Charter-House at London, is a noble foundation; but the house neither of that, Christ-Church, nor anything of the kind at Rome or Venice, comes up to the magnificence of this building; which I suppose is owing to Dr. Balcanqual, his executor, who was a great architect, was Dean of Rochester, and helped King James the Sixth to write his Basilicon Doron, and was left in full power by Mr. Herriot to build this hospital, which he hath done more like a princely palace than a habitation for necessitous children....

To the north of Herriot's work, from whence its fine avenue ascends, and to the west of the Cowgate, is the Grass-Market, like Smithfield at London, where they sell their horses, corn and hay, and is as spacious as Smithfield is; and from it is the West Port or Gate, out of which is a large suburb, as it is at most of the others. The City of Edinburgh is a good English mile from the Palace to the Castle in a direct line; and taking in the suburbs called the West-Port, Bristol, Paterrow, Pleasants, Canongate, and Calton, may be four miles in circumference.

This Grass-Market, or Smithfield, lies directly under the Castle, which is built on a high rock at the west end of the city, and over-looks and commands it. The rock on which this castle is built is inaccessible on all sides, except just the front from the town, which rises by an easy ascent on the ridge of the hill all the way from the Palace: However, this front is secured by a half-moon, at least 200 feet perpendicularly high, well stored with artillery, besides other lower works towards the gate, that make it impregnable. There is also a royal palace in this castle, finely built of free-stone, with very noble apartments; in one of which, King James the sixth of Scotland, and first of England, was born. You may imagine the prospect, very delicious and unbounded from such a height as this; for you not only see all Edinburgh under you, but the whole course of the firth from the Bass to Stirling; the coasts of Fife on the other side of the sea, and many score miles into the country.

FOOTNOTES:

Edinburgh appeared much like this during the first half of the eighteenth century.

Tron.

Gueldres.

Advocates' Library.

Fleurs-de-lis.

See p. 18.

Bristo.

Potterrow.

Pleasance.

THE JACOBITE ATTEMPT OF 1719

Source.—*A Fragment of a Memoir of Field-Marshal James Keith, written by himself, 1714-1734*, p. 35. (Edinburgh: Spalding Club, 1843.)

... To explain the reasons that now carried me to Spain, its necessary to go back to the month of August of this year, when the English, without any previous declaration of war, or even any good ground for it, had attacked the King of Spain's fleet on the coast of Sicily, and entirely ruined it, which so exasperated the Cardinal Alberoni, who then governed Spain with the title of first Minister, that he resolv'd to assist King James, and so revenge himself on the Whigs, who had been the occasion of the breach of faith he complained of.... One difficulty still remain'd,—which was to get the chiefs of the King's friends, who were in France, advertised of this, which the Cardinal desired me to undertake. The Earl Marischal had brought with him from the Duke of Ormonde a little billet containing these words—"Pray have entire confidence in the bearer," and signed Ormond, to be given to him who should be sent; and with this and about 18,000 crowns, I set out from Madrid the 19 of February, and three days after arrived at St. Sebastian, where I deliver'd 12,000 crowns to the Prince Campo Florido, for the equipment of the frigats destin'd for Scotland, and with the little money which remain'd entered France privately....

All things being now ready, we embark'd the 19th of March in a small barck of about 25 tunns, in the mouth of the Seine, and shaped our course to pass betwixt Dover and Calais, and so round the Orkneys to the Isle of Lewis, which was our place of rendezvous; but the wind continuing at east forced us the Friday after, March 24, to alter our course, and stand away for St. George's Channel, or the back of Ireland, as we should think best.... From thence we stood for Cape Clear and the west coast of Ireland, and after favourable but blowing weather, arrived the 4 of April, N.S. in the isle of Lewis, where we enquired if no ship had touched there lately from Spain, or if there was no particular news in the country; but finding them ignorant of any thing that could give us light into what we wanted to be informed of, we remain'd there some days, and at last had accounts that two frigats were come to an anchor on the other side of the island, on which I went with all haste there, not doubting but it was those we were longing for. I found them already sailed, but a gentleman of the country informed me that they were the same, and were gone some miles farther to Stornoway, the only toun or rather village on all the island. I went the same night there, and found them in the harbour at an anchor, and the men still aboard....

The Marquesses of Seafort and Tullibardine came and joined us next day, and in the evening held a council of war to resolve what was to be done. The

Earl Marischal first asked to know what commissions each had, that the command might be regulated, and Lord Tullibardine not owning his late commissions, the command remain'd in him as eldest Major General. It was then disputed whether it was fit to go immediately to the main land of Scotland, or to continue in the island where we were till we had advice of the Duke of Ormonde's landing in England. This last party was much insisted on by Lord Tullibardine and Glenderuel, but all the rest being against it, because we might easily be block'd up in the isle by two or three of the enemies ships, it was resolved to follow the project which the Earl Marischal had proposed to the Cardinal, to land as soon as possible in Scotland, and with the Spaniards and Highlanders who should first join us, march straight to Inverness, in which there were not above 300 of the enemies foot, who would be in no condition to oppose us, and to remain there till we should be joined by such a body of horse and foot as should put us in a condition of marching to the more southern parts of the Kingdom. The council of war being at an end, the Spanish troops were order'd to debark that they might refraich themselves after a voyage of 42 days, and it was resolved to sail for the main land three days after....

We had no sooner debarked the troops and ammunition, than the Earl Marischal and Brigadier Campbel proposed marching straight to Inverness with the Spaniards and 500 Highlanders, whom the Marquess of Seafort promised to give us, to surprise the enemies garison, who as yet had no accounts of us; but the same demon who had inspired them with the design of staying in the Lewis, hinder'd them from accepting this proposition. We were all in the dark what could be the meaning of these dilatory proceedings, which was discover'd to be the effects of the measures they had already taken, for before the Earl Marischal's arrival, they (not knowing but that he might have a commission superior to the Marquess of Tullibardine's) had wrote letters in a circular manner to most of their friends, acquainting them that it was the King's intentions that no body should take arms till the Spanish troops were landed in England; and therefore the Marquess declared that till then he would not stir from where he was, nor even allow any detachments to be made; and some days after, finding that we had still no accounts of the Duke of Ormonde, nor of any movement in England, he proposed that without further delay we should embark aboard the same vessels and return to Spain, from which with great difficulty he was dissuaded.

But the Earl Marischal, fearing that he might renew the same design in case the news we expected was long a coming, declared to him the day after that he was resolved to send the two fregats immediately back to Spain, they being no longer in safety where they were, for being already discover'd, it was natural to believe that the Government of England would immediately send ships to block them up, or to intercept them in their passage home, and in spight of all the arts they used to detain them, three days after they sailed; and indeed just in time, for not a week after their departure arrived three English men of war, much superior to ours both in force and equipage, who, finding we had put most of our ammunition and provisions into an old castel, situate on the shore, under the guard of a detachment of 45 Spaniards, immediately began to batter it from the three ships, and the same night obliged them to surrender prisoners of war.

Our ships were no sooner sailed than the Marquess of Tullibardine began to think of other measures. His retrait out of the island was now impracticable in the manner he had designed it, and now he resolved to draw what ships he could together, but it was too late; he had given the enemy time to draw troops not only from the remote parts of the Kingdom, but even from Holland. The regiments of Kapell, May, and Sturler, were already arrived, and his circular letters had given those who were not very willing an excellent excuse, he himself having already wrote to them that they should not take arms.

Our affairs were in this condition, when we received the news, of the entire dispersion of the Duke of Ormond's fleet; but at the same time our friends assured us that all diligence was using in Spain to put it in a condition to sail again that same spring. This left us still some hopes, and therefore we order'd the gentlemen who were nearest us to assemble their vassalls, but this last accident had disheartned them, that not above a thousand men appeared, and even those seemed not very fond of the enterprize.

The enemy was by this time within three days march of us, with four regiments of foot, and a detachment of a fifth, and 150 dragoons, and waited only for the provisions which was necessary to be carried along (into a country full of mountains and possessed by the enemy,) to march to attack us in our post which, by the situation, was strong enough had it been well defended; our right was cover'd by a rivulet which was difficult to pass, and our left by a ravine, and in the front the ground was so rugged and steep that it was almost impossible to come at us. However, the tenth of June the enemy appear'd at the foot of the mountain, and after having reconnoitred the ground he attacked a detachment we had posted on our right on the other side of the rivulet commanded by Lord George Murray, who not being succour'd as he ought, was obliged to retire, but without any loss. At the same time our center was attacked and forced with very little loss on either side; and after a skirmish of about three hours, in which not above a hundred men were killed or wounded on both sides, and of distinction only the Marquess of Seafort wounded, our troops were forced to retire to the top of the mountain, whose height hinder'd the enemies pursuit. By this time it was night, which gave the chiefs of our party time to consult what was to be done in this urgency, and on considering that they had neither provisions nor ammunition, that the few troops they had had behaved in a manner not to give great encouragement to try a second action, it was resolved, that the Spaniards should surrender, and the Highlanders disperse. Don Nicolas Bolano, who commanded the detachment of the regiment of Galicia, offer'd to attack the enemy once more; but the general officers judging the attempt in vain, the first resolution was followed, and accordingly next morning the Spaniards surrender'd on condition their baggage should not be plunder'd, and every body else took the road he liked best. As I was then sick of a feavour, I was forced to lurck some months in the mountains, and in the beginning of September having got a ship, I embarcked at Peterhead, and 4 days after landed in Hollande at the Texel.

FOOTNOTES:

1718.

1719.

On the mainland.

This was the Battle of Glenshiel.

ENGLAND AND SCOTLAND CONTRASTED
(1725)

Source.—*A Journey through Scotland, in familiar Letters from a Gentleman here, to his Friend Abroad*, p. 269, by J. Macky. Second edition. (London: 1729.)

There is no nation where a man hath fairer play for his liberty, than in Scotland: Here are no Sheriffs Officers, and Marshal's men, that will whip you off the street at London, and run you into a spunging-house at once; but here if you owe money, you are summoned to show cause why you don't pay it; which if you don't do, you have six days allowed you before a caption comes out against your person; which is executed by these messengers only, who are all put in by the Lord Lion, and wear a greyhound on a green ribbon, as a badge, when they are in the execution of their office.

The ladies dress as in England, with this difference, that when they go abroad, from the highest to the lowest, they wear a plaid, which covers half of the face, and all their body. In Spain, Flanders, and Holland, you know the women go all to church and market, with a black mantle over their heads and body: But these in Scotland are all striped with green, scarlet, and other colours, and most of them lined with silk; which in the middle of a church, on a Sunday, looks like a *parterre de fleurs*.

I have been at several consorts of musick, and must say, that I never saw in any nation an assembly of greater beauties, than those I have seen at Edinburgh. The ladies are particular in a stately firm way of walking, with their joints extended, and their toes out: But I cannot say, that the common people are near so clean or handsome as the English. The young ladies are all bred good housewives; and the servant-maids are always kept at some work here: The spinning-wheels, both for woollen and linnen, are always going in most houses; and a gentleman of a good estate is not ashamed to wear a suit of cloaths of his lady's and servants' spinning. They make a great deal of linnen all over the Kingdom, not only for their own use, but export it to England, and to the Plantations. In short, the women are all kept employed, from the highest to the lowest of them.

But the men here are not so usefully employed as in England: There the production of every county is improved by joint-stocks amongst the inhabitants of the several counties. Iron-works, lead-works, manufactories, and every thing else that may conduce to the common welfare of the nation, are set on foot, and carried on. But here, altho their rivers plentifully abound with salmon for exportation, their coasts with white fish and herrings, more than any other in Europe; yet the gentry, or landed men, never concern themselves about it, as a thing below them; and leave those improvements to burghers of towns, who, for want of a sufficient stock, are not able to carry it on.

Indeed, the nobility have of late run into parking, planting, and gardening, which are great improvements of their estates; but what is this to the bulk of a nation, which (if encouraged) hath as many natural commodities for exportation as any whatsoever, and more than South-Britain? But a finer education than what is necessary for trade, hath been, in imitation of the French, the misfortune of this kingdom; but perhaps the union with England may open their eyes to their own interest.

The language of the Low-Countries of Scotland is the same with that which is spoken all over England; only an Englishman will understand a Scotchman better by his writing than speaking; for the difference in the pronunciation of the vowels, which are the same in writing, makes a great alteration in speaking.

The Scots pronounce the five vowels, a, e, i, o, u, just as the French, Germans, and Italians do; and the English, according to that pronunciation, make them œ, i, y, o, u. This difference of sound in the vowels, makes a great one in the pronunciation.

The Highlanders have a language of their own, which the Irish own to be the purest of that Irish which they spake in the province of Ulster in Ireland; which is also spoken in the greatest purity in the Western Islands that lie between Scotland and Ireland: They being an unmixed people, have preserved that language and the dress better than the Irish have done, who have been over-run with Danes, English, etc.

FOOTNOTES:

About.

The Lyon King-at-Arms.

THE MALT TAX (1725)

Source.—*The Lockhart Papers: containing Memoirs and Commentaries upon the Affairs of Scotland from 1702 to 1715, by George Lockhart, Esq., of Carnwath. His Secret Correspondence with the Son of King James the Second from 1718 to 1728, and his other Political Writings*, vol. ii., p. 134. (London: 1817.)

About the latter end of the year 1724 a resolution passed the House of Commons whereby, instead of the malt tax, six pence per barrel of ale was laid of additional duty on Scotland (and not extended to England) and the premiums on grain exported from thence was taken off. As this was a plain breach of the Union, in so far as it expressly stipulated that there shall be an equality of taxes and premiums on trade, every Scots man was highly enraged at it, for as it was evident that the want of the premiums would effectively stop the exportation of grain, which would thereby become a mere drug, no body could foresee to what height this precedent of taxing Scotland separately from England might afterwards be extended. Tis impossible to express the resentment of the nation at this measure, all parties seemed reconciled and to unite in opposing what was so pernicious to the country in general, and at the same time touched every particular man's copyhold. The King's friends laid hold upon this occasion, and privately, underhand, fomented the bad humour, it not being fit, as indeed there was no need of their distinguishing their zeal at this time. A meeting of the heritors of the shire of Edinburgh was called, where I presented an address to the House of Commons, which being heartily approved of, was signed and next day sent up by an express to London....

These warm addresses and instructions did not a little startle the Scots members of Parliament, and even the Ministry; and there were likewise many private letters written to them by their friends, assuring them of the highest resentment if they did not perform what was desired and expected of them. Had these members been endued with a public spirit and resolution, such applications would have been needless; but as they consisted of a parcel of people of low fortunes that could not subsist without their board-wages (which at ten guineas a week during each session was duly paid them) or mere tools and dependents, it was not to be expected they would act the part which became them for their country's service, and therefore these representations were judged necessary to spur them up to their duty and withal show the Ministry that the people would not behave so tamely as did their mean spirited mercenary representatives, who, perceiving they would lose all their interest and scarce dare venture to return home if they did not follow the instructions given them, made most humble applications to the Ministry, who on the other hand being apprehensive the resentment might be carried to some height, and unwilling, as matters stood in Europe, to embroil themselves, thought it expedient to drop the resolutions above mentioned, (which they at first preferred, because they judged it would be no easy matter to levy the malt tax in Scotland) and agreed with the Scots members to impose threepence per bushel on malt; being but the half of what was laid in England; and a bill was accordingly passed as fast as the forms could possibly allow of, least their constituents should have time to remonstrate against it....

Some little time before the 23rd of June (on which day the malt tax commenced) delegates were sent from most of the considerable touns, to meet and confer with the brewers at Edinburgh, where many proposals were made for eluding the law, to be, as occasions offered, put in practice: the first thing to be guarded against was the dutys of malt stock in hand; and to avoid the heavy penalty of not entering the same, it was resolved to obey the law in that respect, but at the same time not to make payment of the duty thereon, and if the Commissioners of excise sued them, to give over brewing and consequently sink the revenue of excise, which was indeed chiefly aimed at by those who bestirred themselves at this time in behalf of the country, that the Government might perceive they'd lose more of the excise than they could gain by the malt tax: but what alarmed people most was the unreasonable article of surcharge, to be levied proportionately off such as entered and paid the duty of what was malted after 23rd of June, in so far as the clear produce (after deducing the charges of collecting) fell short of 20,000*l.* sterling, whereby those who submitted to the Government and paid the malt tax ran the hazard of making up the deficiencie arising from those who did otherwise, which so startled all the considerable brewers, who generally speaking are also maltsters, that they found it absolutely necessary to malt none after the commencement of this duty.

On the 23rd of June, when the duty took place, the excise officers were obliged to fly out of most of the towns in the western shires, but in Glasgow the resentment ran higher. Daniell Campbell of Shawfeild, who represented that burgh in Parliament, having incurred the hatred of the inhabitants thereof, because he was believed, on too good grounds, to have had the chief hand in giving the Government such informations of the way and manner of trading there, as occasioned a few years ago an act of Parliament, that lay heavily on their tobacco trade, was likewise said and believed to have encouraged to hope there was no difficulty in raising the malt tax; and these joined together rendered him detestable over all the Kingdom, especially at Glasgow, where they threatened to pull down his new built house, whereof he sent notice to Wade at Edinburgh on 21st of June, who thereupon ordered a detachment of foot to march forthwith thither, where they arrived on the 24th at night, but the guard room being unprepared, they put off taking possession of it till next day, the soldiers being dismist to their several private quarters. During the night time a report went about that Daniell Campbell had brought these soldiers to enslave them, whereupon the mob got up and destroyed his house, and had he himself been in town, they had certainly dewitted him. Whilst this was in hand the commanding officer got his men together, took possession of the guard room and drew up before it, and tho he met with no insult but from some boys and women, who threw a few stones at his men, without having previously read the proclamation, as directed by the law on such occasions, he fired allongst the streets, which being full of innocent people that came out of curiosity to know what the matter was, and the windows at the same time crowded with spectators, about 20 men and women were killd dead and many more wounded, some whereof in the streets and others in their houses: the citizens being thereby enraged did ring the fire bell and brake up the magazine, from whence they armed about 400 men. In the mean time the magistrates advised the officer to march off his party, for they could not be protected within the city; on which he made the best of his way to Dumbarton, but not thinking himself safe in that town he retired into the castle. The Glasgow mob pursued him a few miles but could not overtake him.

GENERAL WADE'S ROADS (1726)

Source.—*Letters from a Gentleman in the North of Scotland to his Friend in London*, vol. ii., p. 183, by Captain Burt. Fifth edition. (London: 1822.)

LETTER XXVI. CONCERNING THE NEW ROADS, ETC., 173-.

These new roads were begun in the year 1726, and have continued about eleven years in the prosecution; yet, long as it may be thought, if you were to pass over the whole work (for the borders of it would show you what it was), I make no doubt but that number of years would diminish in your imagination to a much shorter tract of time, by comparison with the difficulties that attended the execution.

But, before I proceed to any particular descriptions of them, I shall inform you how they lie, to the end that you may trace them out upon a map of Scotland; and first I shall take them as they are made, to enter the mountains, viz.—

One of them begins from Crief, which is about fourteen miles from Stirling: here the Romans left off their works, of which some parts are visible to this day, particularly the camp at Ardoch, where the vestiges of the fortifications are on a moor so barren, that its whole form has been safe from culture, or other alteration besides weather and time.

The other road enters the hills at Dimheld, in Athol, which is about ten miles from Perth.

The first of them, according to my account, though the last in execution, proceeds through Glenalmond (which, for its narrowness, and the height of the mountains, I remember to have mentioned formerly), and thence it goes to Aberfaldy; there it crosses the river Tay by a bridge of free-stone, consisting of five spacious arches (by the way, this military bridge is the only passage over that wild and dangerous river), and from thence the road goes on to Dalnachardoch.

The other road from Dunkeld proceeds by the Blair of Athol to the said Dalnachardoch.

Here the two roads join in one, and, as a single road, it leads on to Dalwhinny, where it branches out again into two; of which one proceeds towards the north-west, through Garva Moor, and over the Coriarach mountain to Fort Augustus, at Killichumen, and the other branch goes due-north to the barrack of Ruthven, in Badenoch, and thence, by Delmagary, to Inverness. From thence it proceeds something to the southward of the west, across the island, to the aforesaid Fort-Augustus and so on to Fort-William, in Lochaber.

The length of all these roads put together is about two hundred and fifty miles....

In the summer seasons, five hundred of the soldiers from the barracks, and other quarters about the Highlands, were employed in those works in different stations, by detachments from the regiments and Highland companies.

The private men were allowed sixpence a day, over and above their pay as soldiers: a corporal had eight-pence, and a sergeant a shilling; but this extra pay was only for working-days, which were often interrupted by violent storms of wind and rain, from the heights and hollows of the mountains.

These parties of men were under the command and direction of proper officers, who were all subalterns, and received two shillings and sixpence *per diem*, to defray their extraordinary expence in building huts; making necessary provision for their tables from distant parts; unavoidable though unwelcome visits, and other incidents arising from their wild situation....

The standard breadth of these roads, as laid down at the first projection, is sixteen feet; but in some parts, where there were no very expensive difficulties, they are wider....

The old ways (for roads I shall not call them) consisted chiefly of stony moors, bogs, rugged, rapid fords, declivities of hills, entangling woods, and giddy precipices. You will say this is a dreadful catalogue to be read to him that is about to take a Highland journey. I have not mentioned the valleys, for they are few in number, far divided asunder, and generally the roads through them were easily made.

My purpose now is to give you some account of the nature of the particular parts above-mentioned, and the manner how this extraordinary work has been executed; and this I shall do in the order I have ranged them as above.

And first, the stony moors. These are mostly tracts of ground of several miles in length, and often very high, with frequent lesser risings and descents, and having for surface a mixture of stones and heath. The stones are fixed in the earth, being very large and unequal, and generally are as deep in the ground as they appear above it; and where there are any spaces between the stones, there is a loose spongy sward, perhaps not above five or six inches deep, and incapable to produce any thing but heath, and all beneath it is hard gravel or rock....

Here the workmen first made room to fix their instruments, and then, by strength, and the help of those two mechanic powers, the screw and the lever, they raised out of their ancient beds those massive bodies, and then filling up the cavities with gravel, set them up, mostly end-ways, along the sides of the road, as directions in time of deep snows, being some of them, as they now stand, eight or nine feet high. They serve, likewise, as memorials of the skill and labour requisite to the performance of so difficult a work....

Now that I have no further occasion for any distinction, I shall call every soft place a bog, except there be occasion sometimes to vary the phrase.

When one of these bogs has crossed the way on a stony moor, there the loose ground has been dug out down to the gravel, or rock, and the hollow filled up in the manner following, viz.—

First with a layer of large stones, then a smaller size, to fill up the gaps and raise the causeway higher; and, lastly, two, three, or more feet of gravel, to fill up the interstices of the small stones, and form a smooth and binding surface. This part of the road has a bank on each side, to separate it from a ditch, which is made without-side to receive the water from the bog, and, if the ground will allow it, to convey it by a trench to a slope, and thereby in some measure drain it....

The objections made to these new roads and bridges, by some in the several degrees of *condition* among the Highlanders, are in part as follow: viz.—

I. These chiefs and other gentlemen complain, that thereby an easy passage is opened into their country for strangers, who, in time, by their suggestions of liberty, will weaken that attachment of their vassals which it is so necessary for them to support and preserve. That their fastnesses being laid open, they are deprived of that security from invasion which they formerly enjoyed. That the bridges, in particular, will render the ordinary people effeminate, and less fit to pass the waters in other places where there are none. And there is a pecuniary reason concealed, relating to some foreign courts, which to you I need not explain.

II. The middling order say to them the roads are an inconvenience, instead of being useful, as they have turned them out of their old ways; for their horses being never shod, the gravel would soon whet away their hoofs, so as to render them unserviceable; whereas the rocks and moor-stones, though together they make a rough way, yet, considered separately, they are generally pretty smooth on the surface where they tread, and the heath is always easy to their feet....

III. The lowest class, who, many of them, at some times cannot compass a pair of shoes for themselves, they alledge, that the gravel is intolerable to their naked feet; and the complaint has extended to their thin brogues. It is true they do sometimes, for these reasons, go without the road, and ride or walk in very incommodious ways.

FOOTNOTES:

Dunkeld.

SCOTTISH GARDENING (1735)

Source.—*Letters of John Cockburn of Ormistoun to his Gardener, 1727-1744*, p. 22. Edited by James Colville, M.A., D.Sc. (Edinburgh: Scottish Historical Society, 1904.)

3 June, 1735.

CHARLES.—I have had none from you since my last. We have this day a great deal of soft rain, which if with you will do great service to forward both Grass and Corn and may secure many of the weak rooted trees planted last Winter and also make your lay'd trees strike root if well earthed.

This I design chiefly for some thoughts about improving of your father's Garden and land of which if you go right you'l turn a good deal off into Kitchen and Orchard Garden. In doing of which I still think you might have made more progress last Winter and by so doing you might have made a beginning in drawing the people towards a better taste in Garden stuff, which tho' you had made no other profit directly, yet that, if you had saved yourself only, as to the expence, would have been getting [profit], as it would have encreased the demand next year.... Your father's Garden is well sheltered by the houses and rising Ground from the one hand and by the high hedge of the other, and he has water at hand. So he may raise any thing in it the climate will allow of. He has crowded it with fruit trees, too thick even for them to bear as they would, espicially when a little older, as in that warm place they advance very fast. By this he loses the undergrowth also, by which he might make double what he makes by the fruit from the trees, espicially they being of the most common fruit, which would answer as well in the most exposed part of his field. So warm a lying spot should either have been employed entirely in doubled crops for a Kitchen, or, if for fruit, it should have been in kinds every spot won't produce, and for that reason yielded more. I incline to think mulberys would have done of either side the walk at the lower end, as being warm and covered from all severe weather. If so, one tree of them would have yielded as much money as half a dozen of the common apples now in it, and would have taken no more room than one of the present. I am convinced that if Mulberys will do any where in Scotld. they will there, it being entirely covered from Weather and yet open to the Sun, except in so far as shaded by apple trees.... What I aim at is to turn your ground to the best and most proper uses, the warmest and best to what requires it, and the common coarse fruits or herbs to places where they will do and the nicer won't....

Depend upon it there are people in Eden. who have taste, and if you can once get into the custom of some who have it, will put others upon enquiring where they had good things, and this will hold in your herbs etc. as well as in your Fruit. Do you think it possible that there are not Families and Taverns in Eden. that would give reasonably for young pease and Beans in July and Augt if they could get them. Suppose now you sent a dish of young pease or Beans to any of your Customers when only old are to be had, and desire them to let their acquaintances know you can furnish the like, don't you think they would go off, or if you got into the custom of such as Mrs. Thom, who keeps a Tavern, do you believe she would not find people who would be glad of them, and so would take from you. Possibly they may not give such a price as just when first coming in, but if you get a price you can afford them at, it does your business.... People would presently come to distinguish as they came in to buy when Garden stuff was first introduced. But our people are lazie, and saying no body will buy and no body will distinguish, is chiefly owing to the want of activity, Industry and care in providing at all or good of their kinds, and bustling a little to introduce and get Customers at first. We are glad of all excuses for our sleeping on in poverty and our old jog trott. How shall things be carried to Eden. and no body will buy in the country are often very good difficulties and convenient enough excuses, wherein excuse is wanted. I don't know if you have a Carrier at Orm: but I am convinced one who understood his business, would get Employment for a Cart such as the Higlers to the Gardiners who come to Covent Garden use. They would carry things cool and clean, and one man with two horses in such a Cart, would carry in as much as four Carriers with 4 horses carry in our common way and if you put your things up in Baskets carefully as Gardiners do here, by which they'l not be wet, Bruised or Broiled in the Sun, the Cart being covered as the Garden Stuff commonly is, in carrying to Eden. Even care in this will make them fresher and better than what is now to be had there.

HAMPSTEAD, *3ᵈ June*, 1735.

FOOTNOTES:

His gardener's name was Charles Bell.

Edinburgh.

Ormiston.

Costermongers.

THE PORTEOUS RIOTS (1736)

Source.—*Autobiography of the Rev. Dr. Alexander Carlyle, Minister of Inveresk, 1722-1770*, p. 33. (Edinburgh and London: 1860.)

I was witness to a very extraordinary scene that happened in the month of February or March 1736, which was the escape of Robertson, a condemned criminal, from the Tolbooth Church in Edinburgh. In these days it was usual to bring the criminals who were condemned to death into that church, to attend public worship every Sunday after their condemnation, when the clergyman made some part of his discourse and prayers to suit their situation; which, among other circumstances of solemnity which then attended the state of condemned criminals, had no small effect on the public mind. Robertson and Wilson were smugglers, and had been condemned for robbing a custom-house, where some of their goods had been deposited; a crime what at that time did not seem, in the opinion of the common people, to deserve so severe a punishment. I was carried by an acquaintance to church to see the prisoners on the Sunday before the day of execution. We went early into the church on purpose to see them come in, and were seated in a pew before the gallery in front of the pulpit. Soon after we went into the church by the door from the Parliament Close, the criminals were brought in by the door next the Tolbooth, and placed in a long pew, not far from the pulpit. Four soldiers came in with them, and placed Robertson at the head of the pew, and Wilson below him, two of themselves sitting below Wilson, and two in a pew behind him.

The bells were ringing and the doors were open, while the people were coming into the church. Robertson watched his opportunity, and, suddenly springing up, got over the pew into the passage that led in to the door in the Parliament Close, and, no person offering to lay hands on him, made his escape in a moment—so much the more easily, perhaps, as everybody's attention was drawn to Wilson, who was a stronger man, and who, attempting to follow Robertson, was seized by the soldiers, and struggled so long with them that the two who at last followed Robertson were too late. It was reported that he had maintained his struggle that he might let his companion have time. That might be his second thought, but his first certainly was to escape himself, for I saw him set his foot on the seat to leap over, when the soldiers pulled him back. Wilson was immediately carried out to the Tolbooth, and Robertson, getting uninterrupted through the Parliament Square, down the back stairs, into the Cowgate, was heard of no more till he arrived in Holland. This was an interesting scene, and by filling the public mind with compassion for the unhappy person who did not escape, and who was the better character of the two, had probably some influence in producing what followed; for when the sentence against Wilson came to be executed a few weeks thereafter, a very strong opinion prevailed that there was a plot to force the Town Guard, whose duty it is to attend executions under the order of a civil magistrate.

There was a Captain Porteous, who by his good behaviour in the army had obtained a subaltern's commission, and had afterwards, when on half-pay, been preferred to the command of the City Guard. This man, by his skill in manly exercises, particularly the golf, and by gentlemanly behaviour, was admitted into the company of his superiors, which elated his mind, and added insolence to his native roughness, so that he was much feared and hated by the mob of Edinburgh. When the day of execution came, the rumour of a deforcement at the gallows prevailed strongly; and the Provost and Magistrates (not in their own minds very strong) thought it a good measure to apply for three or four companies of a marching regiment that lay in the Canongate, to be drawn up in the Lawnmarket, a street leading from the Tolbooth to the Grassmarket, the place of execution, in order to overawe the mob by their being at hand. Porteous, who it is said, had his natural courage increased to rage by any suspicion that he and his Guard could not execute the law, and being heated likewise with wine—for he had dined, as the custom then was, between one and two—became perfectly furious when he passed by the three companies drawn up in the street as he marched along with his prisoner.

... The street is long and wide, and there was a very great crowd assembled. The execution went on with the usual forms, and Wilson behaved in a manner very becoming his situation. There was not the least appearance of an attempt to rescue; but soon after the executioner had done his duty, there was an attack made upon him, as usual on such occasions, by the boys and blackguards throwing stones and dirt in testimony of their abhorrence of the hangman. But there was no attempt to break through the guard and cut down the prisoner. It was generally said that there was very little, if any, more violence than had usually happened on such occasions. Porteous, however, inflamed with wine and jealousy, thought proper to order his Guard to fire, their muskets being loaded with slugs; and when the soldiers showed reluctance, I saw him turn to them with threatening gesture and an inflamed countenance. They obeyed, and fired; but wishing to do as little harm as possible, many of them elevated their pieces, the effect of which was that some people were wounded in the windows; and one unfortunate lad, whom we had displaced, was killed in the stair window by a slug entering his head. His name was Henry Black, a journey man tailor, whose bride was the daughter of the house we were in. She fainted away when he was brought into the house speechless, where he only lived till nine or ten o'clock. We had seen many people, women and men, fall in the street, and at first thought it was only through fear, and by their crowding on one another to escape. But when the crowd dispersed, we saw them lying dead or wounded, and had no longer any doubt of what had happened. The numbers were said to be eight or nine killed, and double the number wounded; but this was never exactly known.

This unprovoked slaughter irritated the common people to the last; and the state of grief and rage into which their minds were thrown, was visible in the high commotion that appeared in the multitude.... The sequel of this affair was, that Porteous was tried and condemned to be hanged; but by the intercession of some of the Judges themselves, who thought his case hard, he was reprieved by the Queen-Regent. The Magistrates, who on this occasion, as on the former, acted weakly, designed to have him removed to the Castle for greater security. But a plot was laid and conducted by some persons unknown with the greatest secrecy, policy, and vigour, to prevent that design, by forcing the prison the night before, and executing the sentence upon him themselves, which to effectuate cost them from eight at night till two in the morning; and yet this plot was managed so dexterously that they met with no interruption, though there were five companies of a marching regiment lying in the Canongate.

This happened on the 7th of September, 1736; and so prepossessed were the minds of every person that something extraordinary would take place that day, that I, at Prestonpans, nine miles from Edinburgh, dreamt that I saw Captain Porteous hanged in the Grassmarket. I got up betwixt six and seven, and went to my father's servant, who was thrashing in the barn which lay on the roadside leading to Aberlady and North Berwick, who said that several men on horseback had passed about five in the morning, whom having asked for news, they replied there was none, but that Captain Porteous had been dragged out of prison, and hanged on a dyer's tree at two o'clock that morning.

This bold and lawless deed not only provoked the Queen, who was Regent at the time, but gave some uneasiness to Government. It was represented as a dangerous plot, and was ignorantly connected with a great meeting of zealous Covenanters, of whom many still remained in Galloway and the west, which had been held in summer, in Pentland Hills, to renew the Covenant. But this was a mistake; for the murder of Porteous had been planned and executed by a few of the relations or friends of those whom he had slain; who, being of a rank superior to mere mob, had carried on their design with so much secrecy, ability, and steadiness as made it be ascribed to a still higher order, who were political enemies to Government.

THE "CAMBUSLANG WARK" (1742)

Source.—*The Statistical Account of Scotland, drawn up from the communications of the ministers of the different parishes*, vol. v., p. 266, by Sir John Sinclair, Bart. (Edinburgh: 1793.)

Statistical Account of Cambuslang.

In the statistical account of this parish, it will doubtless be expected, that some mention should be made of those remarkable religious phenomena, which took place under Mr. M'Culloch's ministry, commonly called "Cambuslang conversions." In treating of this subject, it will be proper to give a brief historical view, first of the facts, and then of the opinions entertained concerning them.

The kirk of Cambuslang being small and in bad repair, the minister, when the weather was favourable, used to preach in a tent, erected close by a rivulet, at the foot of a bank or brae near the kirk; which is still called "the preaching or conversion brae."... Towards the end of January, 1742, two persons, Ingram More, a shoemaker, and Robert Bowman, a weaver, went through the parish, and got about 90 heads of families to subscribe a petition, which was presented to the minister, desiring that he would give them a weekly lecture.... On Monday, 15th February, and the two following days, all the fellowship meetings in the parish convened in one body in the minister's house, and were employed for many hours in fervent prayer for the success of the gospel, and for an outpouring of the Holy Spirit in their bounds, as in other places abroad: The next day, being Thursday 18th February, nothing remarkable happened during the lecture, except that the hearers were apparently all attention; but when the minister in his last prayer expressed himself thus: "Lord who hath believed our report; and to whom is the arm of the Lord revealed? where are the fruits of my poor labours among this people?" several persons in the congregation cried out publicly, and about 50 men and women came to the minister's house, expressing strong conviction of sin, and alarming fears of punishment. After this period, so many people from the neighbourhood resorted to Cambuslang, that the minister thought himself obliged to provide them with daily sermons or exhortations, and actually did so for 7 or 8 months.

The way in which the converts were affected, for it seems they were all affected much in the same way, though in very different degrees, is thus described. They were seized all at once, commonly by something said in the sermons or prayers, with the most dreadful apprehensions concerning the state of their souls, insomuch that many of them could not abstain from crying out in the most public and dreadful manner, ... The agony under which they laboured, was expressed not only by words, but also by violent agitations of body; by clapping their hands and beating their breasts; by shaking and trembling; by faintings and convulsions; and sometimes by excessive bleeding at the nose. While they were in this distress, the minister often called out to them, not to stifle or smother their convictions, but to encourage them; and, after sermon was ended, he retired with them to the manse, and frequently spent the best part of the night with them in exhortations and prayers. Next day before sermon began, they were brought out, commonly by More and Bowman, and having napkins tied round their heads, were placed all together on seats before the tent, where they remained sobbing, weeping, and often crying aloud, till the service was over. Some of those who fell under conviction were never converted; but most of those who fell under it were converted in a few days, and sometimes in a few hours.... From the time of their conviction to their conversion, many had no appetite for food, or inclination to sleep, and all complained of the severity of their sufferings during that interval.

This singular work soon became public, made a great noise, and brought vast numbers of people from all quarters.... Among those who resorted to Cambuslang on this occasion, there were many of the most popular ministers in Scotland; ... Mr Whitefield, who had been in England for several months, did not arrive till June. The sacrament was given twice in the space of 5 weeks, viz. on 11th July and 15th August. Immense multitudes of hearers and spectators were present at both, but especially at the last. On the Sunday, besides the tent at the foot of the brae above described, where the sacrament was dispensed, other two tents were erected. At each of these there was a very great congregation. Mr Whitefield, who was accustomed to numerous audiences, supposed, that at the three tents, there were upwards of 30,000 people; a greater number probably than was ever seen on any other sacramental occasion. Most of the above mentioned ministers and others were assistants at this solemnity. Four preached on the fast-day, 4 on Saturday, probably 14 or 15 on Sunday, and 5 on Monday. There were 25 tables, about 120 at each, in all 3,000 communicants. A great many of these came from Glasgow and the neighbourhood, about 200 from Edinburgh, about 200 from Kilmarnock, about 200 from Irvine and Stewarton, and some from England and Ireland.... The Cambuslang work continued for about six months, that is, from the 18th February till the second communion.

FOOTNOTES:

George Whitefield, the friend of Wesley.

THE "FORTY-FIVE."
A. PRINCE CHARLES LANDS IN SCOTLAND (JULY 1745).

Source.—*Culloden Papers: comprising an Extensive and Interesting Correspondence from the Year 1625 to 1748 ... the Whole published from the Originals in the Possession of Duncan George Forbes, of Culloden, Esq.*, p. 203. (London: 1815.)

The Lord President to Mr. Pelham.

2nd Aug^t, 1745.

DEAR SIR,

In a state of profound tranquillity, we have been alarmed with advices, which are said to have been received at London, of intended invasions; and particularly of a visit which the Pretender's eldest son is about to make to us, if he has not already made it. These informations, particularly as to the visit just mentioned, I must confess, have not hitherto gain'd my belief. This young gentleman's game seems at present to be very desperate in this country; and, so far as I can learn, there is not the least apparatus for his reception, even amongst the few highlanders who are suspected to be in his interest. However, as, when so much is at stake, no advice, how improbable soever, is to be neglected, I have (our session being now over) resolved to make my accustomed journey northwards a little earlier than usual; to the end that, though my fighting days are over, I may give some countenance to the friends of the government, and prevent the seduction of the unwary, if there should be any truth in what is reported.

Mr. Normand MacLeod to the Lord President.

MY DEAREST LORD,

To my no small surprise, it is certain that the Pretended Prince of Wales is come on the coast of South Uist and Barra, and has since been hovering on parts of the coast of the main land that lies between the point of Airdnamurchan and Glenelg; he has but one ship, of which he is aboard; she mounts about 16 or 18 guns. He has about thirty Irish or French officers with him, and one Sheridan, who is called his Governor. The Duke of Athol's brother is the only man of any sort of note (that once belonged to this country) that I can hear of that's alongst with him. His view, I need not tell you, was, to raise all the Highlands to assist him, etc. Sir Alex. Macdonald and I, not only gave no sort of countenance to these people, but we used all the interest we had with our neighbours to follow the same prudent method; and I am persuaded we have done it with that success, that not one man of any consequence benorth the Grampians will give any sort of assistance to this mad rebellious attempt. How far you think we acted properly, I shall long to know; but this is certain, we did it as our duty and for the best; for in the present situation of affairs in Europe, I should have been sorry to see any thing like disaffection to the Government appear, tho' ever so trivial; or that there was occasion to march a single company to quell it, which now I hope and dare say there is not....

I ever am, most faithfully, Yours,
NORMAND MACLEOD.

DUNVEGAN, *3rd Aug*, 1745.

B. Raising the Prince's Standard (August)

Source.—*Memorials of John Murray of Broughton, sometime Secretary to Prince Charles Edward, 1740-1747*, p. 168. Edited by Robert Fitzroy Bell. (Edinburgh: Scottish Historical Society, 1898.)

The Chevalier was now preparing to come to the rendezvous at Glenphinan the 18 of Agust, and accordingly arrived there the 17th in the evening with only three companys of Clanronalds followers. The next day Locheil joined him with seven hundred and fifty men besides double officers, and Mcdonald of Keppoch arrived in the afternoon with his regiment consisting of about three hundred. In less than an hour after the whole were drawn up, and the Royal Standart display'd by the D. of A[thole] when the Chevalier made them a short but very pathetick speech. Importing that it would be no purpose to declaim upon the justice of his father's title to the throne to people who, had they not been convinced of it, would not have appeared in his behalf, but that he esteemed it as much his duty to endeavour to procure their welfare and happiness as they did to assert his right, that it was chiefly with that view that he had landed in a part of the Island where he knew he should find a number of brave gentlemen fired with the "noble example of their predecessors, and jealous of their own and their country's honour, to join with him in so glorious an enterprise, with whose assistance and the protection of a just God who never fails to avenge the cause of the injured, he did not doubt of bringing the affair to a happy issue...."

Everything now being prepared for the Chevalier's departure, upon the 21st he moved from the place of rendezvous to the head of Locheil, about nine miles from Fort William, and as the difficulty of finding horses and the badness of the roads in this country were equally unsurmountable, of twenty large swevel guns he made twelve be buried in a bog about a mile from the place where he first erected his standard. He had no sooner arrived at the above mentioned place than he received intelligence of G[eneral] C[ope] having moved north ward and at the same time had a copy of the proclamation sent which had been ishued by order of the Lords Justices, affixing thirty thousand pound upon his head....

Upon seeing it he was heard to say that tho it was true that a reward had been likewise set upon his father's head in the year 1715, that yet he imagined that in proportion as the world grew in politeness they had done so in humanity, that it were unjust to call the ancients rude and savage etc., when no example could be given of their taking so mean and unmanly a way to get rid of their enemy. That he should have been far from ever thinking of such a device to exterminate the E[lector]s family did his success depend upon it, but at the same time he could not in justice to him self get by offering the same reward in his turn. Tho if he could allow himself to think that any of his friends could be so abandoned as to be guilty of so execrable a deed for the sum proposed, that he would alter the sum to thirty pound instead of thirty thousand, and then ordered a proclamation of the same nature to be drawn, which was signed and published two days after.

FOOTNOTES:

= avoid.

C. THE CAPTURE OF EDINBURGH (SEPTEMBER)

Source.—*The History of the Rebellion in the year 1745*, p. 86, by John Home, Esq. (London: 1802.)

The night between the 15th and 16th of September passed without disturbance. Six or seven hundred men, consisting of the Trained Bands, the Edinburgh volunteers, and some volunteers who came in from the towns of Musselburgh and Dalkeith, were upon guard at the different gates of the city. On Monday the 16th the rebels advanced slowly towards Edinburgh, giving time for the terror of their approach to operate upon the minds of unwarlike citizens, in a divided city. Between ten and eleven o'clock in the forenoon, a message was delivered from the young Pretender to the people of Edinburgh, acquainting them that if they would admit him peaceably into the city, they should be civilly dealt with, if not they must lay their account with military execution.

Instantly the clamour rose, and crowds of people ran about the streets crying out, that it was madness to think of resistance, since the dragoons were fled; and some of them meeting Provost Stuart, as he returned from the West Port (where he had gone to give orders after the retreat of the dragoons), followed him to the Parliament Square, beseeching him not to persist in defending the town, for if he did they should all be murdered. The Provost reprimanded them; and went to the Goldsmiths' Hall, where the Magistrates and Town Council were assembled, with a good many of the inhabitants. A deputation was sent to the Justice Clerk, the Advocate, and the Solicitor, to entreat that they would come and assist the Council with their advice. The deputies returned, and reported that all these gentlemen had left the town. Provost Stuart then sent for the captains of the volunteers, and the Trained Bands, and desired to have their opinion concerning the defence of the town. The officers said very little, and seemed to be at a loss what opinion to give; other people in the meeting made speeches for and against the defence of the town, not without reproach and abuse on both sides. The crowd encreased to such a degree, that it became necessary to adjourn to a larger place, and the meeting adjourned to the New Church Aisle, which was immediately filled with people, the most part of whom called to give up the town; that it was impossible to defend it. Those who attempted to speak against the general opinion, were borne down with noise and clamour....

About ten o'clock at night the deputies returned, and brought a letter in answer to the message sent by them.

"His Royal Highness the Prince Regent thinks his Manifesto, and the King his father's declaration already published, a sufficient capitulation for all His

Majesty's subjects to accept of with joy. His present demands are to be received into the city, as the son and representative of the King his father, and obeyed as such when there, His Royal Highness supposes, that since the receipt of his letter to the Provost, no arms or ammunition have been suffered to be carried off or concealed, and will expect a particular account of all things of that nature. Lastly, he expects a positive answer, before two o'clock in the morning, otherwise he will think himself obliged to take measures conform.

"At Gray's Mill, 16th September, 1745. By his Highness's command.

When this letter was read, Provost Stuart said, there was one condition in it, which he would die rather than submit to, which was receiving the son of the Pretender as Prince Regent; for he was bound by oath to another master. After long deliberation it was determined to send out deputies once more, to beg a suspension of hostilities till nine o'clock in the morning, that the Magistrates might have an opportunity of conversing with the citizens, most of whom were gone to bed. The deputies were also instructed to receive an explanation of what was meant by receiving Charles as Prince Regent.

About two o'clock in the morning the deputies set out in a hackney coach for Gray's Mill; when they arrived there they prevailed upon Lord George Murray to second their application for a delay; but Charles refused to grant it; and the deputies were ordered in his name to get them gone.

The coach brought them back to Edinburgh, set them down in the High-Street, and then drove towards the Canongate. When the Nether Bow port was opened to let out the coach, 800 Highlanders, led by Cameron of Locheil, rushed in and took possession of the city.

It was about five o'clock in the morning when the rebels entered Edinburgh. They immediately sent parties to all the other gates, and to the town guard, who making the soldiers upon duty prisoners, occupied their posts as quietly as one guard relieves another. When the inhabitants of Edinburgh awakened in the morning, they found that the Highlanders were masters of the city.

FOOTNOTES:

Who had been sent to parley with the rebels.

D. Prince Charles at Holyrood (September)

Source.—*The History of the Rebellion in the year 1745*, p. 99, by John Home, Esq. (London: 1802.)

About ten o'clock the main body of the rebels marching by Duddingston (to avoid being fired upon by the Castle) entered the King's Park, and halted in the hollow between the hills, under the peak called Arthur's seat. By and by Charles came down to the Duke's Walk, accompanied by the Highland Chiefs, and other commanders of his army.

The Park was full of people (amongst whom was the author of this history,) all of them impatient to see this extraordinary person. The figure and presence of Charles Stuart were not ill suited to his lofty pretensions. He was in the prime of youth, tall and handsome, of a fair complexion; he had a light coloured periwig with his own hair combed over the front: he wore the Highland dress, that is a tartan short coat without the plaid, a blue bonnet on his head, and on his breast the star of the order of St. Andrew. Charles stood some time in the park to show himself to the people; and then, though he was very near the palace, mounted his horse, either to render himself more conspicuous, or because he rode well, and looked graceful on horseback.

The Jacobites were charmed with his appearance: they compared him to Robert the Bruce, whom he resembled (they said) in his figure as in his fortune. The Whigs looked upon him with other eyes. They acknowledged that he was a goodly person; but they observed, that even in that triumphant hour, when he was about to enter the palace of his fathers, the air of his countenance was languid and melancholy: that he looked like a gentleman and man of fashion, but not like a hero or conqueror. Hence they formed their conclusions that the enterprize was above the pitch of his mind; and that his heart was not great enough for the sphere in which he moved. When Charles came to the palace, he dismounted, and walked along the piazza, towards the apartment of the Duke of Hamilton. When he was near the door, which stood open to receive him, a gentleman stepped out of the crowd, drew his sword, and raising his arm aloft, walked up stairs before Charles. The person who enlisted himself in this manner, was James Hepburn of Keith, whose name will be mentioned again more than once....

The Highlanders, when they entered the town in the morning, had secured the Heralds and Pursuivants: at midday they surrounded the Cross with a body of armed men, and obliged the Heralds to proclaim King James, to read the Commission of Regency, and the Declaration, dated at Rome, in December 1743, with a Manifesto in the name of Charles Prince Regent, dated at Paris, 16th of May, 1745. An immense multitude witnessed this ceremony, which was performed at noon. The populace of a great city, who huzza any thing that brings them together, huzzaed; and a number of ladies in the windows strained their voices with acclamation, and their arms with waving white handkerchiefs in honour of the day. These demonstrations of joy, amongst people of condition, were chiefly confined to one sex; few gentlemen were to be seen on the streets, or in the windows; and even amongst the inferior people, many shewed their dislike by a stubborn silence.

FOOTNOTES:

On September 17.

E. THE BATTLE OF PRESTONPANS (SEPTEMBER)

Source.—*Memorials of John Murray of Broughton, sometime Secretary to Prince Charles Edward*, 1740-1747, p. 198. Edited by Robert Fitzroy Bell. (Edinburgh: Scottish Historical Society, 1898.)

On thursday the 19th, in the evening, the Chevalier had certain intelligence that G[ll] Cope had marched that morning from Dunbar, and was to encamp that night at Haddingtown, upon which he immediately gave orders for the guards of the City to retire early next morning, and he went himself that night to Duddingston....

In obedience to the orders given on the morning of the twentieth the guards retired from the City and joined the army at Duddingston, and brought alongst with them some surgeons, with whom the army was then very ill provided, and some coaches and chaises were likewise ordered for the conveniency of the wounded, so certain was the prospect of a battle, and even a successful one. Thus all things being prepared about nine in the morning, after receiving an exact account of the number of the enemy taken at Haddington, the Chevalier put himself at the head of his small army, drawing his sword, said with a very determined countenance, Gentlemen, I have flung away the scabbard, with God's assistance I don't doubt of making you a free and happy people, Mr. Cope shall not escape us as he did in the Highlands, and then began his march, ordering the few horse, he then had, not above fifty in number, to advance at some small distance in front, and to detach a few to discover the enemy's march. In this manner, with the Camerons in front, he marched in good order, crossing Musselburgh bridge by Pinky park wall. By this time the party of horse sent intelligence that G[ll] Cope was nigh to Tranent, from which the Chevalier conjectured that he would engage him on the muir to the west ward of that village, and therefore quickened his march to prevent his gaining the brow of Carberry hill before him, but before he had near reached the top of the hill he was told that Sir John had marched to the left, and posted himself in a low ground betwixt Preston and Seaton. This naturally led him to imagine that he intended to avoid coming to action; and made him determine, if possible, to attack him the same day. With this view he advanced to the hill and drew up his army opposite to G[ll] Cope, who was formed in the low ground before mentioned in two lines, with the two regiments of Dragoons on his wings. So soon as the Chevalier had taken a view of the enemy he judged it impossible to attack them in the post they was then in, having a deep ditch in their front which runs along the high road, where he must have sustained great loss before he could pass it; but being determined that at no rate the enemy should give him the slip a second time, he ordered a detachment to take possession of the

Church yard which commanded their camp on the left, and as that seemed the only side where it was possible to come at them, he enquired if there was none in the army acquainted with the country to know if the ground would allow him to attack them on the left. There happened to be a gentleman in the army of that county, who told him that there was only one pass on the left whereby not guarded he could come to them, upon which he ordered it to be reconnoitred, and finding it neglected he ordered a detachment of 500 men to be posted upon the high road to the west of Preston to prevent the enemys retiring by that road to Edinburgh, and recalling the detachment from the Church yard he marched his army eastward by the town of Tranent, and drew up in one line opposite to the flank of the enemy, who upon that motion made a half wheel to face him, expecting, as it was imagined, that he then designed to attack them, and which L. G. M—y proposed, as the Highlanders were then full of spirits, and above all things desirous to engage; but the night being then far advanced, the Chevalier thought it better to delay coming to an engagement till next morning, not knowing what might be the consequence of a rencounter in the night should the enemy, if beat, rally and come upon him while in confusion and not able to get his people together, knowing how difficult it was to keep irregular troops together in a body after an action, so resolved to delay it till early next morning, and ordered his army to halt upon the ground about three or four hundred yards from the enemy, and to continue under arms to be ready to march upon a minutes warning.

They accordingly lay close in order of battle the whole night without the least whisper or noise to be heard, while G^{ll} Cope made some fires in his camp and threw a few shells, which did no hurt. Having continued in this position for some time, he was informed that the detachment of five hundred Atholl men which he had posted upon the west side of the village of Preston had rejoined the army; this made him very uneasy least the enemy had filed off during the night by that road and had taken possession of the City of Edin^r, to prevent which and to intercept the runaways had enduced him to make that disposition. He at first seemed resolved to make them return, but when he reflected that their march, if discovered by the enemy, might induce them to believe it was the whole army, and occasion them to alter their disposition or occasion any confusion or distrust amongst his own people, he judged it safer and better to put up with the disappointment and continue the rest of his plan, tho he could not help complaining that his orders had been neglected in so material a point.

Notwithstanding this *faux pas*, he kept in very high spirits the rest of the night, laying on the ground without any covering but his plaid, and in the morning, about an hour before daylight, made his army, guided by the gentleman above mentioned, march from the left in three columns, making the left of the first line the right of the army for the attack, which motion, tho perhaps irregular, was yet necessary, and executed with so much order and silence that the small body of horse posted in the rear knew nothing of their march; the officer on duty, either through forgetfulness or that he thought they could be of no service, neglected to give them orders to march. In this order he marched to the enemy, passing a deep bog with out the least observation. The right, composed of the M^cdon^{ds} of Glengarry and Clanronald, was commanded by the D. of P., and the left, commanded by L.G.M., which had made the right the preceding day, consisted of the Camerons and Steuarts of Appin. The third column, which was made up of the Atholl men, was commanded by My L[ord] N[airn]. So soon as the two first columns had passed the bog, they formed and marched straight to the enemy, who by this time had formed and presented themselves in the same order of battle they had appeared the day before. By this time the third column had likewise passed and formed themselves about four score yards in the rear of the first line; rather too near, if the ground would have allowed of a more regular disposition. The left, when pretty near the enemy, finding themselves outwinged, made a motion to front the artillery, which occasioned a gap in the centre, but marching up briskly, they received one fire of the cannon, which did little hurt, and then receiving a fire from the foot, they gave a loud huzza, returning the fire, upon which Gairdner's dragoons run off, and the Highlanders, throwing away their muskets, attacked the foot with incredible impetuosity, who immediately gave ground. Upon the left of the enemy the resistance, if such behaviour merits the name, was much less, for before the D. of P. was within three score yards of them, Hamilton's dragoons began to reel and run off before they could receive his fire; the foot likewise fired too soon, and almost all turned their backs before the Highlanders could engage them with their swords. In a few minutes the rout was total; the dragoons on the right run off by the high road through the town of Preston, and those on the left by the shore towards the east; the few of the foot that saved themselves escaped by Preston Park, the wall of which had been broke down the day before by G^{ll} Cope's orders. All the baggage of the army was placed in a yard upon the left of their army, guarded by two companies of L. Lowdon's regiment, where so soon as the action was over, Capt Bazil Cochran of Coll. Lees was sent by L.G.M. to tell them that if they would immediately surrender as prisoners of war they should be used as such, if not, they would be immediately attacked and no quarter given, upon which they readily gave up their arms.

FOOTNOTES:

Lord George Murray.

Duke of Perth.

Lord George Murray.

Lee's Regiment, the 44th, now the Essex Regiment.

F. "JOHNNIE COPE."

Source.—*The Jacobite Songs and Ballads of Scotland from 1688 to 1746*, p. 181. Edited by Charles Mackay, LL.D. [London and Glasgow: 1861.]

SIR JOHN COPE trode the north right far,Yet ne'er a rebel he cam naur,Until he landed at Dunbar,Right early in the morning.Hey, Johnnie Cope, are ye wauking yet?Or are ye sleeping, I would wit?O haste ye, get up, for the drums do beat:O fye, Cope, rise in the morning!

He wrote a challenge from Dunbar,"Come fight me, Charlie, an ye daur;If it be not by the chance of war,I'll give you a merry morning."Hey, Johnnie Cope, etc.

When Charlie look'd the letter upon,He drew his sword the scabbard from,"So heaven restore me to my own,I'll meet you, Cope, in the morning."Hey, Johnnie Cope, etc.

Cope swore with many a bloody word,That he would fight them gun and sword;But he fled frae his nest like a weel-scar'd bird,And Johnnie he took wing in the morning.Hey, Johnnie Cope, etc.

It was upon an afternoon,Sir John march'd into Preston town,He says, "My lads, come lean you down,And we'll fight the boys in the morning."Hey, Johnnie Cope, etc.

But when he saw the Highland ladsWi' tartan trews and white cockades,Wi' swords and guns, and rungs and gauds,O Johnnie took wing in the morning.Hey, Johnnie Cope, etc.

On the morrow when he did rise,He look'd between him and the skies;He saw them wi' their naked thighs,Which fear'd him in the morning.Hey, Johnnie Cope, etc.

O then he fled into Dunbar,Crying for a man of war;He thought to have pass'd for a rustic tar,And gotten awa in the morning.Hey, Johnnie Cope, etc.

Sir John then into Berwick rade,Just as the deil had been his guide;Gi'en him the world, he wadna staidT' have foughten the boys in the morning.Hey, Johnnie Cope, etc.

Said the Berwickers unto Sir John,"O what's become of all your men?""In faith," says he, "I dinna ken;I left them a' this morning."Hey, Johnnie Cope, etc.

Says Lord Mark Kerr, "Ye are na blate,To bring us the news o your ain defeat,I think you deserve the back o' the gate;Get out o' my sight this morning."Hey, Johnnie Cope, etc.

FOOTNOTES:

Written after the Battle of Prestonpans.

Cudgels.

Rods.

Bashful.

Own.

G. INVASION OF ENGLAND (NOVEMBER-DECEMBER)

Source.—*Memorial: Lochgary to Glengary*, printed as a postscript to W. B. Blaikie's *Itinerary of Prince Charles Edward Stuart from his Landing in Scotland, July, 1745, to his Departure in September, 1746*, p. 116. (Edinburgh: Scottish Historical Society, 1897.)

About the beginning of Novr the Prince called a council o' war, wherein H.R.H. determined to march into England with the forces he then had, and not to wait those who were coming up, but ordered them to follow.

We marched on without halt till we came to Brampton, near Carlile, where the Prince rested with part o' the army, and order'd the siege of Carlile, which surrender'd after four days' siege. The next day after the surrender, the Prince enter'd the town with his whole army, where H.R.H. remain'd some days. From thence he march'd straight with his whole army till he arrived at Darby, where he rested two days; and H.R.H. called a council o' war, and finding most of the private people of the army's opinion to be rather to retreat than goe forward (tho' at the same time H.R.H.'s opinion and inclination was to goe forward), he agreed to a retreat. Consequently, we began our retreat next day. Lord George Murray, who always had the rear, chose our regiment for the rearguard, tho' it was not our turn. When we came to Kendal, we had accounts of the enemy's being close in our rear; and our regiment's having the rearguard, and likewise the charge of the artillery. The Prince marched on with the army till they arrived at Penrith, and the weather very terrible, the rear could not reach Chap that night, which is halfway twixt Penrith and Kendal. Lord George took up our quarters in a little villiage, where we rested that night on our arms, without thro'ing a stitch of cloaths, as we were sure the enemy was very near us. Next day we marched by daylight, and for want of proper horses the artillery was very fashious, and a last load with cannon shot happening to break on the road, upon Lord George's giving a hearty dram to the men, they carried, some one, some two, some three of the shot, with all their arms and acuterments. All this day some of the enemy's horse were in our rear, but made no attack. This night we came to Chap, and after placing our guards and sentinelles, Lord George, the other gentlemen, and I, took up our quarters about 8 o'clock at night.... By the break o' day Lord George order'd to beat to arms, and order'd the artillery on before. We marched on, expecting every minut the enemy wou'd be up with us, having none with us but your regiment and about one hundred and twenty of Roy Stuart's regiment. About halfway to Penrith, we saw at some distance, to the number of about 5 or 600 horse, whom we took to be part of our own army; but upon coming near us they made a form to attack us. These were militia sent to intercept our march; but by a detachment we sent to attack them giving them a smart fire, which kill'd two or three of them, they were routed, and fled, so we march'd on untill we came to Clifton, within two short miles of Penrith, where the Prince and his army lay. Here Lord George got account that some of the enemy were come to the house of Lowtherhall, about a mile's distance on our left. He desired me to ask the men (as he knew they were fatigued) if they were willing to attack that house. They answer'd me that they were most willing. Upon which we marched and surrounded the house, and only found in it one officer, with a footman of the Duke of Cumberland's, whom he had sent before to take up quarters for him. Upon our return to Clifton, we perceived the enemy to the number of about 3000 horse, advanced by this time within ¼ of a mile of Clifton. Cluny and his McPhersons, to about the number of three hundred men, happened to be at this village. Lord George ordered them on one post on the side of the road, and our regiment on another on the other side. It was then about nightset, when the enemy, being all horse, dismounted—I can't condescend on their number, being then dark—and attack'd the McPhersons, who received them, and after a close fire for some time on both sides, the enemy were repulsed. Upon this they sent a stronger body to attack us both, which came directly up to us, and it being then quite dark, they coming very close to us, we only heard the noise of their boots, and could plainly discern their yellow belts. We first received their full fire, which did us little damage. We immediately gave them ours, and then attacked them sword in hand, and oblibged them to retreat with a considerable loss.

Lord George then marched with us and the McPhersons into the town, where we found the whole army ready to march for Carlisle, so that we had neither time to refresh ourselves, or men. So you may judge our condition, having marched t[w]o days without resting from Kendal to Penrith, which is long 20 miles, and, without halt, 16 more on to Carlisle, all without any sleep and very little provision; yet we brot all the artillery safe, and lost very few men at the attack at Clifton. I received a small wound there myself in the knee, and no other gentleman touched. We stay'd two days at Carlisle. The third day in the morning by break o' day we marched, expecting surely to meet Cumberland that day to give him battle; but perceiving no enemy, march'd forward, and that night crossed the Esk. H.R.H. continued on his march without any remarkable occurencies till he arrived safe with his army at Glasgow.

FOOTNOTES:

December 6, "Black Friday."

Shap.

I.e., without undressing.

Troublesome.

H. THE BATTLE OF FALKIRK (JANUARY, 1746)

Source.—*The Lockhart Papers: containing ... also Journals and Memoirs of the Young Pretender's Expedition in 1745, by Highland Officers in his Army*, vol. ii., p. 499. (London: 1817.)

On the sixth of January we marched from Glasgow to Cumbernauld and from thence to Falkirk. Next day orders were sent to the army at Perth to join us and with the artillery to invest Stirling Castle. After staying about a week, four of our six Highland regiments which were in England were ordered to march to Linlithgow under night, both to levy the publick money and carry off the provisions which had been ordered to be provided for the English army now convened about Edinburgh under the command of General Hawley who was advancing towards us.... The Duke of Perth commanded the siege of Stirling Castle, the Prince's headquarters being at Bannockburn near Falkirk....

General Hawley (who had been joined by the Argyleshire Highlanders to the number of about twelve hundred under General Campbell) with the Government's troops encamped a little northwest from the toun of Falkirk. The P. finding General Hawley did not move from his camp at Falkirk to attack him, held a council of war, January the seventeenth, about midday, wherein it was resolved to march and attack Hawley. Accordingly we set out in two columns, and under the cover of the Tor wood passed the water of Carron at Dunipace; moving on very quickly to gain the hill above and lying on the south west of Falkirk our two columns kept at an equal distance of about two hundred paces till we came in sight of the enemy about a mile and a half distant from us. At the same time that we began our march Lord John Drummond with most of the horse had gone to reconnoitre the enemy, and made a movement as if he intended to march by the high way through the Tor wood close up to them, and this might occasion what some accounts tell us of General Hawley's perceiving a body of the Highlanders in the Tor wood, took this appearance to be our whole army, and finding they did not advance, allowed his troops to dine in their camp.

But to return to our main body; whilst we were making up towards the hill above Falkirk (as was said) the enemy at last perceived us and immediately their three regiments of dragoons were ordered up to gain the ground upon us and hinder our forming till their foot should form and their cannon be brought up the hill to support them. The P. seeing the intention of the enemy, ordered 1500 or 2000 of his Highlanders, led on by Lord George Murray and Lochiel, to advance and drive the dragoons from the eminence they had possessed, till the main body of our men should come up, and to form the right of our army. This attack upon the dragoons was very quick and regular; as we came within pistolshot the dragoons made up to us at a full trot, thinking to bear us down by their weight, and break us at once, and indeed being well mounted and accoutred they made a glorious show, sufficient to have struck other hearts than ours with a pannick. We received them, however, with a very smart fire, upon which they reeled and broke into several divisions, some falling back upon their own foot on the left, others flying out of the field, whilst one body of them fled off to the right betwixt the front lines of both armies, which by this time were formed.... As the enemy's dragoons rode off to their right betwixt the lines, our men ran eagerly in pursuit of them, but were much surprised to find themselves stopped by our generals and officers, who with difficulty restrained them with their drawn swords and cocked pistols, conjuring them to return to their ground or they would be undone. As the dragoons in their flight betwixt the lines passed by our left wing they could not forbear giving them part of their fire likewise. Our left had not been fully formed when the attack begun on the right; a considerable body of the enemy's horse came up also to attack them, but receiving part of the fire of our left they broke and run off; their infantry coming in upon that side were opposed by some of our battalions, who receiving the enemy's fire went in amongst them sword in hand and drove them down the hill with great impetuosity and slaughter, but not being in sight of our right (by reason of the unevenness of the ground) they made a halt till such time as the two wings should join in the centre and the second line come up. His R. H., whose attention was turned to all quarters observing that our left wing was outlined by the enemy, sent Brigadier Stapleton with the pickets of the Irish Brigade and some other battalions from the second line, which extended our first line and recovered the disorder we were like to be put into. Then our whole army marched down towards the enemy, who were retreating on all sides in great disorder, but by reason of the unevenness of the ground and night coming on with a storm of wind and rain they could not overtake them, as they were positively ordered to keep their ranks. The enemy, finding they could neither possess nor save their camp, set fire to their tents and retreated with great precipitation towards Linlithgow, and were just got to the east end of the toun of Falkirk when Lord John Drummond entered it on that side, Lord George Murray in the middle, and Lochiel in the west end of the toun. We took most of their cannon, ammunition, and baggage which they had not themselves destroyed. We reckoned about seven hundred of the enemy taken prisoners and about six hundred men and between thirty or forty officers killed. We had not above forty men killed on our side, amongst whom were two or three captains and some subaltern officers.

I. RETREAT TO THE NORTH (FEBRUARY TO APRIL, 1746)

Source.—*The Lyon in Mourning: or, a Collection of Speeches, Letters, Journals, etc., relative to the Affairs of Prince Charles Edward Stuart*, vol. i., p. 83, by the Rev. Robert Forbes, A.M., Bishop of Ross and Caithness, 1746-1775. Edited from his manuscript, with a preface by Henry Paton, M.A. (Edinburgh: Scottish Historical Society, 1895.)

Journal by MR. JOHN CAMERON, *Presbyterian Preacher and Chaplain at Fort-William.*

The retreat from Stirling was made with the utmost hurry and confusion. The evening before, Mr. O'Sullivan wrote from Bannockburn to Lord John Drummond ordering him to leave Stirling and cross the Forth by break of day, which order his lordship obeyed, and by 5 in the morning marched. This surprised the Highlanders, to whose officers it appears these orders were not communicate, and made them believe the enemy was near them, which occasioned such an universal consternation that they went from Stirling as everyone was ready, and left most of their baggage, all the cloaths they brought from Glasgow, and some of their arms.

Lochiel, who had been wounded at Falkirk, not being able to ride or walk, went in a chaise with Mrs. Murray, and was driving through St. Ninian's when the church blew up. Some of the stones came very near them. The horses startled and threw Mrs. Murray on the street, where she lay speechless till she was taken up by some of the men. Had there been any intention to blow up the church, doubtless Lochiel, one of their principal officers, and the Secretary's lady had been apprized of it and put on their guard to avoid danger.

When the Prince join'd the body of the army a Council of War was held, in which it was debated whether the army should march in a body to Inverness by Aberdeen or take the Highland road, by which the chiefs could, with the greater ease, get such of their men to rejoin them as had gone home with plunder after the battle of Falkirk, which would considerably increase their army. The low-country men were of the former opinion, the Highlanders of the latter. It was put to the vote, and the latter carried it by a great majority. However, the Prince was positive for the Aberdeen road, with which Lochiel complied. But Cluny, going out, met Mr. Murray, and told him it was surprizing the Prince should be so positive in a thing contrary to reason and his own instinct, especially when a great majority of the Council of War were of another opinion. His expressing himself with a little warmth made Mr. Murray speak to Sir Thomas Sheridan, who went to the Prince and prevailed upon him to agree with what had been the opinion of the Council of War. He marched with the Highlanders the Highland road by Ruthven in Badenoch, to Inverness, where it was resolved to attack Fort Augustus and Fort William. Of either I can give no distinct account, but that the first was taken, and the siege of the other deserted.

Earl Cromertie and others were sent to different countries to cover the rising of some and prevent that of others. This weakened the army, and tho' many joined the day before the battle of Culloden, a great number did not. Earl of Cromertie, tho' many expresses were sent to order his returning to Inverness, in place of doing as commanded, was surprized and taken prisoner; and these that did join were much fatigued. None had got pay after they left Tay bridge in their march north, and they were straightened in provisions for some days before the battle. Cumberland's army was not opposed in passing the Spey, tho' a considerable force had been sent there for that end. The Prince was in danger of being taken at MacIntosh's house, and his safety was chiefly owing to a mistake of Earl of Loudon's men.

FOOTNOTES:

This is incorrect.

J. THE EVE OF CULLODEN (APRIL, 1746)

Source.—*Memoirs of Sir Robert Strange, Knight, and of his Brother-in-Law, Andrew Lumisden, Private Secretary to the Stuart Princes*, vol. i., p. 54, by James Dennistoun, of Dennistoun. (London: 1855.)

Such was the position of my undertaking when, all of a sudden, news was brought to Inverness that the Duke of Cumberland, with his army, had passed the Spey on the 13th of April. The town was in a general alarm, and even in confusion. Nothing was heard but the noise of bagpipes, the beating of drums, and the clash of arms. The field of Culloden was the following day to be the general rendezvous, and every individual betook himself to his corps.

The army was now mustering upon the field, it being the 14th; but unfortunately we had not been joined by a considerable number of our men, who were actually upon their march from different parts of the country, and would have been up in the course of a few days. The whole of the Macphersons, a considerable body of the Frasers, some few of the Macintoshes, in general all the Mackenzies, and several other bodies of men who had been raised in the more northern counties, had all received repeated expresses, and were hastening to join the army. In this situation, divested as it were of part of our numbers, we hourly expected the Duke. He had come on to Nairn on the 14th, and was there halting. There was even no appearance of his moving, the 15th being his birthday. In the afternoon of that day, the Prince had summoned a council of war to be held upon the field, and had proposed a plan of a march under cloud of night, to attack the Duke's army by surprise, and to force his camp. This plan was worthy even of any of the greatest heroes of antiquity, and met with general approbation, particularly amongst the clans. The council remained long in deliberating in what manner it was to be conducted. Two essential things, secrecy and expedition, were the great objects to be observed. There was only one road to Nairn, which was the high road; and this being covered in many places with villages, it was essential to avoid it, to prevent any information being carried to the Duke's army. The next alternative, and indeed the only one, was to attempt a way along the foot of a ridge of mountains which fronted the sea, but had scarcely ever been trod by human foot, and was known by the name of the Moor-road. It would have brought us in upon that part of the enemy's camp from which they could apprehend no danger. It lengthened indeed the road, which, in the sequel, and from the shortness of the night, proved our misfortune.

Before the council broke up, every regiment as it were had his place assigned him in the order of the march. The van was commanded by Lord

George Murray, who, with about one-third of the army, was to have passed the water of Nairn about two miles distant from the town, and who, unexpected by the enemy, was to have invested the Duke's quarters, and to have made him prisoner. The remaining two-thirds, commanded by the Duke of Perth and Lord John Drummond, were to have attacked them from the plain, which, in all probability, would have been carried sword in hand. It is to be remarked that the same army had been already surprised at Falkirk.

Night coming on—and not sooner could the army begin its march, to prevent the country people from being alarmed, or any intelligence being carried to the enemy,—part of our numbers, weak as we were, was under a necessity of being left on the field, in order to save appearances, and light up fires, as had been done the preceding evening, and to prevent stragglers, if any there were, forming unnecessary conjectures. The night was favourable to our wishes, but alas! such a road was never travelled; the men in general were frequently up to the ankles, and the horses in many places extricated themselves with difficulty. In this manner were we retarded almost the whole of the night; notwithstanding of which, an uncommon spirit supported itself throughout the army.

It was now the 16th of April, when day began to break about four in the morning. It was indeed a dreadful knell to us, being as yet above four long miles from Nairn; nor did we know what sort of road we had yet to encounter. Appearances became serious, each was whispering to his neighbour, and, so far as countenances could be descried, disappointment was evidently marked. During this critical moment of suspense, what was to be done? A halt took place; a council was called as soon as the general officers could be got together. The morning was fine, and the day was ushering in apace; it required but little time to deliberate, and finding it impossible to attack the Duke by surprise, it was judged expedient, for the safety of the army, to give up the enterprise, and return to the field of Culloden. Thus were our hopes disappointed. We saw, as it were before us, the glorious prize; but we durst not encounter it, for there is almost a moral certainty that we should have been cut off to a man. The enemy was early in motion, must have seen us at a considerable distance, and received us upon the points of their bayonets.

FOOTNOTES:

Strange, an expert engraver, was printing Jacobite bank-notes.

K. THE BATTLE

Source.—*Idem.*, p. 60.

Let us for an instant review the situation of this army. They had, for many weeks before the battle, been reduced to a short allowance of bread; when I say bread, I mean oatmeal, for they had no other. Must not this have enfeebled their bodies? Their treasury-chest had been nearly exhausted: they had received but little money: of course considerable arrears were owing them. They had passed the 14th and following night under arms upon the field of battle, every instant expecting the Duke. Upon the night of the 15th, which was the eve of the battle, they had performed the march I have described. Judge, then, what was to be expected from such an army, worn out with fatigue, and at this moment short of the common necessaries of life, and outnumbered upwards of two to one by their enemies; for the Duke's army consisted of at least eleven thousand men; that of the Prince did not exceed six, of which we shall find at least a thousand during the action were asleep in Culloden parks. What, then, can justify the deliberate folly and madness of fighting under such circumstances? But our time was come. We were at variance within ourselves: Irish intriguers and French politics were too predominant in our councils. These gentlemen, forsooth, considered themselves as to be but prisoners of war, whilst every other individual were fighting with halters round their necks. General appearances upon the field of battle were much against us. No line was as yet formed; the men were standing in clusters; and stragglers in small numbers were coming up from all quarters. Overpowered with fatigue, they had stopped everywhere on the road, and were now joining the army.

It being determined to give battle to the Duke, no time was now lost in forming the lines, and in making every proper disposition. The right of the army, commanded by Lord George Murray, was composed of his own regiment of Athol, the Camerons, Stuarts of Appin, one battalion of the Frasers, and the Macintoshes. The left wing, commanded by the Duke of Perth, consisted of the MacDonalds of Glengarry, Keppoch, and Clanronald, two companies of MacLeans, two of MacLeods, and the Farquharsons. The second line, commanded by Lord John Drummond and Major-general Stapleton, consisted of the Irish pickets, the regiments of Lord Ogilvy, Lord Lewis Gordon, Duke of Perth, and Lord John Drummond. On the right wing, behind the second line, was a troop of Fitz-James' horse, and on the left part of the horse-guards, Perthshire squadron, and hussars. The regiment of Kilmarnock's foot-guards, and Colonel John Roy Stuart, with such of the men as had no guns, formed a sort of reserve. The Prince, attended by his aides-de-camp, and Lord Elcho's guards, placed himself towards the centre, behind the first line. We had six pieces of cannon; two placed on the right, two on the left, and two in the centre of the front line.

The Duke of Cumberland drew up his army in three lines. The first, commanded by Lieutenant-general the Earl of Albemarle, consisted of the regiments of Burrel, Monro, Scot's Fusiliers, Price, Cholmondley and St. Clair. The second, commanded by Major-general Huske, consisted of the regiments of Wolfe, Ligonier, Sempill, Bligh, and Fleming. The third line, commanded by Brigadier Mordaunt, consisted of the regiments of Blackney, Battereau, Pultney, and Howard. On the right wing were placed Cobham's dragoons, and the half of Kingston's horse; and on the left Ker's dragoons, and the other half of Kingston's horse, with the Campbells of Argyle. Ten pieces of cannon were placed in the first line, two between each regiment, and six pieces in the second line.

The enemy formed at a considerable distance, and marched on in order of battle, outlining us both on the right and on the left. About one o'clock the cannonading began; and the Duke's artillery, being well served, could not fail of doing execution. One of the Prince's grooms, who led a sumpter horse, was killed upon the spot; some of the guards were wounded, as were several of the horse. One Austin, a very worthy, pleasant fellow, stood on my left; he rode a fine mare, which he was accustomed to call his lady. He perceived her give a sudden shrink, and, on looking around him, called out, "Alas! I have lost my lady!" One of her hind legs was shot, and hanging by the skin. He that instant dismounted, and, endeavouring to push her out of the ranks, she came to the ground. He took his gun and pistols out of the holsters, stepped forward, joined the foot, but was never more heard of. The Prince, observing this disagreeable position, and without answering any end whatever, ordered us down to a covered way, which was a little towards our right, and where we were less annoyed with the Duke's cannon; he himself, with his aides-de-camp, rode along the line towards the right, animating the soldiers. The guards had scarce been a minute or two in this position, when the small arms began from the Duke's army, and kept up a constant fire; that instant, as it were, one of the aides-de-camp returned, and desired us to join the Prince. We met him in endeavouring to rally the soldiers, who, annoyed with the enemy's fire, were beginning to quit the field. The right of our army, commanded by Lord George Murray, had made a furious attack, cut their way through Burrel's and Monro's regiments, and had taken possession of two pieces of cannon; but a reinforcement of Wolfe's regiment, etc., coming up from the Duke's second line, our right wing was obliged to give way, being at the same time flanked with some pieces of artillery, which did great execution. Towards the left the attack had been less vigorous than on the right, and of course had made but little impression on the Duke's army; nor was it indeed general, for the centre, which had been much galled by the enemy's artillery, almost instantly quitted the field.

The scene of confusion was now great; nor can the imagination figure it. The men in general were betaking themselves precipitately to flight; nor was there any possibility of their being rallied. Horror and dismay was painted in every countenance. It now became time to provide for the Prince's safety: his person had been abundantly exposed. He was got off the field, and very narrowly escaped falling in with a body of horse, which had been detached from the Duke's left, were advancing with an incredible rapidity, picking up the stragglers, and, as they gave no quarter, were levelling them with the ground. The greater numbers of the army were already out of danger, the flight having been so precipitate. We got upon a rising ground, where we turned round and made a general halt. The scene was, indeed, tremendous. Never was so total a rout—a more thorough discomfiture of an army. The adjacent country was in a manner covered with its ruins. The whole was over in about twenty-five minutes. The Duke's artillery kept still playing, though not a soul upon the field. His army was kept together, all but the horse. The great pursuit was upon the road towards Inverness. Of towards six thousand men, which the Prince's army at this period consisted of, about one thousand were asleep in Culloden parks, who knew nothing of the action till awaked by the noise of the cannon. These in general endeavoured to save themselves by taking the road towards Inverness; and most of them fell a sacrifice to the victors, for this road was in general strewed with dead bodies. The Prince at this moment had his cheeks bedewed with tears; what must not his feeling heart have suffered?

FOOTNOTES:

The Jacobite one.

The hero of Quebec.

L. THE PRINCE A FUGITIVE (APRIL-MAY 1746)

Source.—*The Lyon in Mourning: or, a Collection of Speeches, Letters, Journals, etc., relative to the Affairs of Prince Charles Edward Stuart*, vol. i., p. 367, by the Rev. Robert Forbes, A.M., Bishop of Ross and Caithness, 1746-1775. Edited from his manuscript, with a preface by Henry Paton, M.A. (Edinburgh: Scottish Historical Society, 1895.)

Copy of CAPTAIN O'NEILLE'S *Journal, taken from an attested copy by his name subscribed with his own hand.*

That night the Prince retir'd six miles from the field of battle and went next day as far, and in three days more arrived at Fort Augustus, where he remained a whole day in expectation his troops would have join'd him. But seeing no appearance of it, he went to the house of Invergary and ordered me to remain there to direct such as pass'd that way the road he took. I remained there two days and announc'd the Prince's orders to such as I met, but to no effect, every one taking his own road.

I then followed the Prince, who was so far from making a precipitate retreat [as has been maliciously reported] that he retired by six and six miles and arrived the 28th of April O.S. at Knoidart, where I join'd him next day and gave him an account of the little or no appearance there was of assembling his troops, upon which he wrote circular letters to all the chieftains, enjoining them, by the obedience they owed him, to join him immediately with such of their clans as they could gather; at the same time representing to them the imminent danger they were in if they neglected it. After remaining some days there in hopes his orders would have been obeyed, and seeing not one person repair to him, the extreme danger his person was in, being within seven miles of Lord Loudon, Sir Alexander MacDonald and the MacLeods, it was proposed to evade it by retreating to one of the islands near the continent. After repeated instances of the like nature he reluctantly assented, leaving Mr. John Hay behind to transmit him the answers of his letters, with an account of what should pass, and parted for the Isles in an open fishing boat at eight at night, attended by Colonel O'Sullivan and me only. About an hour after we parted a violent hurricane arose, which drove us ninety miles from our designed port; and next day running for shelter into the Island of North Uist, we struck upon a rock and staved to pieces, and with great difficulty saved our lives. At our landing we were in the most melancholy situation, knowing nobody and wanting the common necessaries of life. After much search we found a little hut uninhabited, and took shelter there, and with a great deal of pains made a fire to dry our cloaths. Here the Prince remained two days, having no other provisions but a few biskets we had saved out of the boat, which were entirely spoiled with the salt water.

As this island belonged to Sir Alexander MacDonald, and not judging ourselves safe, we determined going elsewhere, and by the greatest good fortune, one of our boatmen discovered a boat stranded on the coast, and having with great difficulty launched it into the water, we embarked for the Harris. In our passage we unfortunately met with another storm which obliged us to put into an island near Stornoway.... And meeting with three ships of war we were constrained to put into a desert island where we remained eight days in the greatest misery, having no sustenance but some dried fish that Providence threw in our way in this island. When the ships disappeared we put to sea again, and next morning met with another ship of war just coming out of one of the lochs, who pursued us for near an hour; but the wind rising we made our escape. In the afternoon we arrived at the Island of Benbecula.... Here we remained some days longer, till the Duke of Cumberland having intelligence that the Prince was concealed in the Long Isle, ordered the militia of the Isle of Sky and the Independent Companies to go in search of him. As soon as we had notice of their landing we retreated to an island about twelve miles distance, called Ouya, where we remained till we found they had followed us, and then we went for Loch Boisdale, and stayed there eight days, when Captain Carolina Scott landed within a mile of us, which obliged us to separate, the Prince taking me to the mountains, and O'Sullivan remaining with the boatmen.

FOOTNOTES:

April 16.

A vast exaggeration.

Should be Benbecula.

M. FLORA MACDONALD (JUNE, 1746)

Source.—*The Lyon in Mourning: or, a Collection of Speeches, Letters, Journals, etc., relative to the Affairs of Prince Charles Edward Stuart*, vol. i., p, 296, by the Rev. Robert Forbes, A.M., Bishop of Ross and Caithness, 1746-1775. Edited from his manuscript, with a preface by Henry Paton, M.A. (Edinburgh: Scottish Historical Society, 1895.)

Journal taken from the mouth of MISS FLORA MACDONALD *by* DR. BURTON *of York, when in Edinburgh.*

Miss MacDonald had gone from Sky to Milton in South Uist in order to visit her brother-german, who had about that time taken up house. She had not been long there till Captain O'Neil (by some lucky accident or other) had become acquainted with her. When the Prince was surrounded with difficulties on all hands, and knew not well what to do for his future safety, Captain O'Neil brought Miss MacDonald to the place where the Prince was, and there they concerted the plan. At that time Miss returned to Milton. After Miss MacDonald had (with some difficulty) agreed to undertake the dangerous enterprize, she set out for Clanranald's house, Saturday, June 21st, and at one of the fords was taken prisoner by a party of militia, she not having a passport. She demanded to whom they belonged? And finding by the answer that her step-father was then commander, she refused to give any answers till she should see their captain. So she and her servant, Neil MacKechan, were prisoners all that night.

Her stepfather, coming next day, being Sunday, she told him what she was about, upon which he granted a passport for herself, a manservant (Neil MacKechan), and another woman, Bettie Burk, a good spinster, and whom he recommended as such in a letter to his wife at Armadale in Sky, as she had much lint to spin. If her stepfather (Hugh MacDonald of Armadale) had not granted Miss a passport, she could not have undertaken her journey and voyage. Armadale set his stepdaughter at liberty, who immediately made the best of her way to Clanranald's house and acquainted the Lady Clanranald with the scheme, who supplied the Prince with apparel sufficient for his disguise, viz. a flower'd linen gown, a white apron, etc., and sent some provisions along with him.

During Miss MacDonald's stay at Clanranald's house, which was till the Friday, June 27th, O'Neil went several times betwixt the Prince and Miss, in which interval another scheme was proposed, that the Prince should go under the care of a gentleman to the north ward, but that failing them, they behoved to have recourse to that agreed upon before; and accordingly Lady Clanranald, one Mrs. MacDonald, O'Neil, Miss Flora MacDonald, and her servant, Neil MacKechan, went to the place where the Prince was, being about eight Scotch miles. He was then in a very little house or hut, assisting in the roasting of his dinner, which consisted of the heart, liver, kidneys, etc., of a bullock or sheep, upon a wooden spit. O'Neil introduced his young preserver and the company, and she sat on the Prince's right hand and Lady Clanranald on his left. Here all dined very heartily....

When all were gone who were not to accompany the Prince in his voyage to the Isle of Sky, Miss MacDonald desired him to dress himself in his new attire, which was soon done, and at a proper time they removed their quarters and went near the water with their boat afloat, nigh at hand for readiness to embark in case of an alarm from the shore. Here they arrived, very wet and wearied, and made a fire upon a rock to keep them somewhat warm till night. They were soon greatly alarmed by seeing four wherries full of armed men making towards shore, which made them extinguish their fire quickly, and to conceal themselves among the heath....

At eight o'clock, June 28th, Saturday, 1746, the Prince, Miss Flora MacDonald, Neil MacKechan, etc., set sail in a very clear evening from Benbecula to the Isle of Sky. It is worth observing here that Benbecula is commonly reckoned a part of South Uist, they being divided from one another by the sea only at high water, which then makes a short ferry betwixt the two; but at low water people walk over upon the sand from the one to the other.

They had not rowed from the shore above a league till the sea became rough, and at last tempestuous, and to entertain the company the Prince sung several songs and seemed to be in good spirits.

In the passage Miss MacDonald fell asleep, and then the Prince carefully guarded her, lest in the darkness any of the men should chance to step upon her. She awaked in a surprise with some little bustle in the boat, and wondered what was the matter, etc....

From hence they rowed on and landed at Kilbride, in Troternish, in the Isle of Sky, about twelve miles north from the above-mentioned point. There were also several parties of militia in the neighbourhood of Kilbride. Miss left the Prince in the boat and went with her servant, Neil MacKechan, to Mougstot, Sir Alexander MacDonald's house, and desired one of the servants to let Lady Margaret MacDonald know she was come to see her ladyship in her way to her mother's house. Lady Margaret knew her errand well enough by one Mrs. MacDonald, who had gone a little before to apprize her of it.

As Mr. Alexander MacDonald of Kingsburgh was accidentally there, Lady Margaret desired him to conduct the Prince to his house; for it is to be remarked that Lady Margaret did not see the Prince in any shape. Kingsburgh sent a boy down to the boat with instructions whither to conduct the Prince about a mile, and he (Kingsburgh) would be there ready to conduct him. Then Kingsburgh took some wine, etc., to refresh the Prince with, and set forwards for the place of rendezvous, leaving Miss MacDonald with Lady Margaret at Mougstot, where the commanding officer of the parties in search of the Prince was, and who asked Miss whence she came, whither she was going, what news? etc., all which Miss answered as she thought most proper, and so as to prevent any discovery of what she had been engaged in.

Lady MacDonald pressed Miss very much in presence of the officer to stay, telling her that she had promised to make some stay the first time she should happen to come there. But Miss desired to be excused at that time, because she wanted to see her mother, and to be at home in these troublesome times. Lady Margaret at last let her go, and she and Mrs. MacDonald above mentioned set forwards with Neil MacKechan and said Mrs. MacDonald's maid and her man-servant. They overtook the Prince and Kingsburgh. Mrs. MacDonald was very desirous to see the Prince's countenance; but as he went along he always turned away his face from Mrs. MacDonald to the opposite side whenever he perceived her endeavouring to stare him in the countenance. But yet she got several opportunities of seeing his face, though in disguise, which the maid could not help taking notice of, and said she had never seen such an impudent-looked woman, and durst say she was either an Irish woman or else a man in a woman's dress. Miss MacDonald replied she was an Irish woman, for she had seen her before. The maid also took notice of the Prince's awkward way of managing the petticoats, and what long strides he took in walking along, etc., which obliged Miss MacDonald to desire Mrs. MacDonald (they being both on horseback), to step a little faster and leave those on foot, because, as there were many parties of militia in the great roads, it was necessary for the Prince to cross the country, and it was not proper to let Mrs. MacDonald's man or maid servant see it. So on they went, and the Prince and Kingsburgh went over the hills and travelled south-south-east till they arrived at Kingsburgh's house, which was about twelve o'clock at night, and they were very wet....

The day was far advanced before he set out, and when he arrived at a wood side (as the affair had been concerted), not far from Kingsburgh, he changed his apparel once more and put on the Highland dress Kingsburgh had furnished him with. Then Kingsburgh sent a guide with him to Portree, thro' all byways, while Miss MacDonald went thither on horseback by another road, thereby the better to gain intelligence and at the same time to prevent a discovery. They were very wet, it having rained very much. Here he only dried his clothes, took some little refreshment, and staid about two hours.

Hither Kingsburgh had sent to prepare a boat, and to have it ready to convey the Prince to the place where he wanted to be at, not allowing the people about Portree in the meantime to know anything about the person's being the Prince whom they were to receive and to take care of. Young MacLeod of Raaza came with Malcolm MacLeod to conduct the Prince over to the Island of Raaza. The Prince was very uneasy he had not a MacDonald to conduct him still. He left Portree on Tuesday, the 1st of July, and landed that very same day at a place called Glam in Raaza.

Miss MacDonald took leave of the Prince at Portree, and from thence went to her mother, after a fatiguing journey cross the country. She never told her mother, or indeed anybody else, what she had done.

FOOTNOTES:

The Prince.

N. CHARLES AT CLUNY'S "CAGE" (SEPTEMBER, 1746)

Source.—*The History of the Rebellion in the year 1745*, Appendix No. xlvi., p. 377, by John Home, Esq. (London: 1802.)

Cluny's account of Locheil and himself after the Battle of Culloden: of their meeting with Charles; and the extraordinary habitation called the Cage, where Charles lived with them, till he received notice that two French frigates were arrived at Lochnanuagh.

After the fatal catastrophe of the Highland army at Culloden, upon the 16th of April, 1746, they meant to make head again about Cluchnicarry, till, upon Lord Loudon's approach with an army, the few that had got together were made to disperse. Locheil being then bad of his wounds, was obliged to shift from his own country to the Braes of Rannoch, near which, about the 20th of June, in a hill called Benouchk, Cluny Macpherson met him, and Sir Stuart Threipland, physician, who attended him for the cure of his wounds. Cluny brought them from thence to Benalder, a hill of great circumference in that part of Badenoch next to Rannoch, and his own ordinary grassings; where they remained together, without ever getting any certain notice of what had become of the Prince for near three months, when they received the agreeable news of his being safe at Locharkaik....

The Prince lay the first night at Corineuir, after his coming to Badenoch, from which he was conducted next day to Mellanauir, a shealing of very narrow compass, where Locheil, with Macpherson of Breakachie, Allan Cameron, his principal servant, and two servants of Cluny were at the time. It cannot but be remarked, that, when Locheil saw five men approaching under arms, being the Prince, Lochgary, Dr. Cameron, and two servants, taking the five men to be of the army or militia, which lay encamped not above four or five miles from them, and were probably in search of them; as it was in vain to think of flying, Locheil at the time being quite lame, and not in any condition to travel, much less to run away; it was resolved that the enemy, as they judged them to be, should be received with a general discharge of all the arms; in number twelve firelocks and some pistols.... But the auspicious hand of Almighty God ... prevented those within from firing at the Prince with his four attendants; for they came at last so near that they were known by those within.... Locheil then ushered him into his habitation, which was indeed but a very poor one. The Prince was gay, and in better spirits than it was possible to think he could have been, considering the many disasters, disappointments, fatigues and difficulties, he had undergone. His Royal Highness, with his retinue, went into the hut; and there was more meat and drink provided for him than he expected. There was plenty of mutton, an anker of whisky, containing twenty Scots pints, some good beef sausages made the year before, with plenty of butter and cheese, besides a large well cured bacon ham. Upon his entry, the Prince took a hearty dram, which he sometimes called for thereafter, to drink the healths of his friends. When some minced collops were dressed with butter, in a large sauce-pan, which Locheil and Cluny always carried about with them, being the only fire vessel they had, His Royal Highness eat heartily, and said with a very cheerful countenance: "Now, gentlemen, I live like a Prince:" though at the same time he was no otherwise entertained than eating his collops out of the pan, with a silver spoon....

The day after Clunie arrived, he thought it time to remove from Mellanauir, and took the Prince about two miles further into Benalder, to a little sheil called Uiskchibra, where the hut or bothie was superlatively bad and smoky; yet His Royal Highness put up with everything. Here he remained for two or three nights; and then removed to a very romantic habitation, made for him by Clunie, two miles further into Benalder, called the Cage; which was a great curiosity, and can scarcely be described to perfection. It was situated in the face of a very rough, high and rocky mountain, called Letternilichk, still a part of Benalder, full of great stones and crevices, and some scattered wood interspersed. The habitation called the Cage, in the face of that mountain, was within a small thick bush of wood. There were first some rows of trees laid down, in order to level a floor for the habitation; and as the place was steep, this raised the lower side to an equal height with the other; and these trees, in the way of joists or planks, were levelled with earth and gravel. There were betwixt the trees, growing naturally on their own roots, some stakes fixed in the earth, which, with the trees, were interwoven with ropes, made of heath and birch twigs, up to the top of the Cage, it being of a round or rather oval shape; and the whole thatched and covered over with fog. This whole fabric hung, as it were, by a large tree, which reclined from the one end, all along the roof to the other, and which gave it the name of the Cage, and by chance there happened to be two stones at a small distance from one another, in the side next the precipice, resembling the pillars of a chimney where the fire was placed. The smoke had its vent out here, all along the face of the rock, which was so much of the same colour, that one could discover no difference in the clearest day. The Cage was no larger than to contain six or seven persons; four of whom were frequently employed playing at cards, one idle looking on, one baking, and another firing bread and cooking. Here His Royal Highness remained till the 13th of September, when he was informed that the vessels for receiving and carrying him to France were arrived at Lochnanuagh. The Prince set out immediately; and travelling only by night, arrived at Borodale, near Lochnanuagh, on the 19th of September, and embarked there on the 20th.

FOOTNOTES:

Grazings.

Moss.

CPSIA information can be obtained
at www.ICGtesting.com
Printed in the USA
LVHW041247280423
745505LV00004B/533